BLACK&DECKER®

HERE'S HOW...

CERAMIC TILE

Easy, Elegant Makeovers

Creative Publishing
international

MINNEAPOLIS, MINNESOTA
www.creativepub.com

Contents

1 Purchasing Materials . . .4

2 Cutting Tile 6

3 Mixing & Using Mortar 12

4 Tools for Cutting Tile . . .14

5 Tools for Setting & Grouting Tile 15

6 Preparation Materials . .16

7 Materials for Setting & Grouting Tile 17

8 Installing Underlayment 18

9 Installing & Finishing Wallboard 22

10 Installing Cementboard 24

11 Installing Wall Membranes 24

12 Laying Out Floor Designs 28

13 Laying Out
Wall Designs 35

14 Installing a
Tile Floor 40

15 Installing a Glass
Mosaic Floor 48

16 Building a Tiled
Shower Base 52

17 Installing a
Tile Wall 60

18 Tiling a Kitchen
Backsplash 68

19 Building a Tiled
Tub Deck 72

20 Building a Tile
Countertop 78

21 Tilng Concrete
Steps 88

APPENDIX:

Glossary 94

1. Purchasing Materials

Before you can select or purchase materials, you'll need to figure out exactly what you need and how much. Start by drawing a room layout, a reference for you and for anyone advising you about the project.

To estimate the amount of tile you need for a floor project, calculate the square footage of the room and add five percent for waste. For example, in a 10-foot × 12-foot room, the total area is 120 square feet. (12' × 10' = 120 sq. ft.). Add five percent, 6 square feet, for breakage and other waste (120 × .05 = 6 sq. ft.). You need to purchase enough tile to cover 126 square feet.

Tile cartons generally indicate the number of square feet one carton will cover. Divide the square footage to be covered by the square footage contained in a carton in order to determine the number of cartons required for your floor project. For example, if a carton holds 10 square feet, you will need 13 cartons to cover the 10 × 12 floor in our example.

Estimating tile for a wall project is slightly more complex. Start by deciding how much of each wall will be tiled. In a shower, plan to tile to at least 6" above the showerhead. It's common for tile to extend 4 feet up the remaining walls, although it's possible and sometimes very attractive for full walls to be tiled.

To calculate the amount of field tile required, measure each wall and multiply the width times the height of the area to be covered. Subtract the square footage of doors and windows. Do this for each wall, then add all the figures together to calculate the total square footage. Add five percent for waste. Calculate the number of cartons necessary (square footage of the project divided by the square footage contained in a carton).

Trim for floors and walls is sold by the lineal foot. Measure the lineal footage and calculate based on that. Plan carefully—the cost of trim tile adds up quickly.

Before buying the tiles, ask about the dealer's return policy. Most dealers allow you to return unused tiles for a refund. In any case, think of it this way: buying a few too many tiles is a small problem. Running out of tiles when the job's almost done could turn into disaster if you can no longer get the tile or the colors don't match.

How to Purchase Materials

Use your room drawing to identify all the types of trim that will be necessary (above). Evaluate the trim available for the various tiles you're considering and select a combination that meets the specifications of your project.

Buy all necessary tile, tools, and materials at once to avoid wasted trips and to make sure all the elements are appropriate for one another and the project.

Design and paint your own custom tiles at many specialty ceramic stores. Order tile of the right size and have them bisque-fired but not glazed. You can then paint or stencil designs on the tile and have them fired. Look in the phone book for specialty ceramic stores.

Mix tile from carton to carton. Slight variations in color won't be as noticeable mixed throughout the project as they would be if the color shifts from one area to another.

2. Cutting Tile

Careful planning will help you eliminate unnecessary cuts, but most tile jobs require cutting at least a few tiles and some jobs require cutting a large number of tiles, no matter how carefully you plan. For a few straight cuts on light- to medium-weight tile, use a snap cutter. If you're working with heavy tile or a large number of cuts on any kind of tile, a wet saw greatly simplifies the job. When using a wet saw, wear safety glasses and hearing protection. Make sure the blade is in good condition and the water container is full. Never use the saw without water, even for a few seconds.

Other cutting tools include nippers, hand-held tile cutters, and rod saws. Nippers can be used on most types of tile, but a rod saw is most effective with wall tile, which generally is fairly soft.

A note of caution: hand-held tile cutters and tile nippers can create razor-sharp edges. Handle freshly cut tile carefully, and immediately round over the edges with a tile stone.

Before beginning a project, practice making straight and curved cuts on scrap tile.

How to Cut Tile

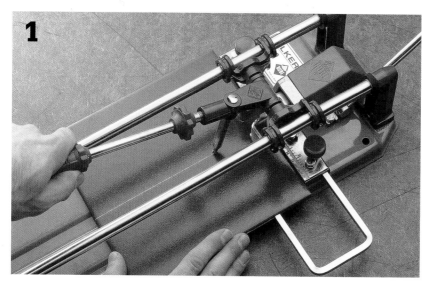

Mark a cutting line on the tile with a pencil, then place the tile in the cutter so the cutting wheel is directly over the line. While pressing down firmly on the wheel handle, run the wheel across the tile to score the surface. For a clean cut, score the tile only once.

Snap the tile along the scored line, as directed by the tool manufacturer. Usually, snapping the tile is accomplished by depressing a lever on the tile cutter.

How to Use a Wet Saw

Individual saws vary, so read the manufacturer's directions for use and make sure you understand them. Refer any questions to the rental center. Wear safety glasses and hearing protection; make sure water is reaching the blade at all times.

Place the tile on the sliding table and lock the fence to hold the tile in place, then press down on the tile as you slide it past the blade.

How to Mark Square Notches

Place the tile to be notched over the last full tile on one side of the corner. Set another full tile against the ½" spacer along the wall and trace along the opposite edge onto the second tile.

Move the top two tiles and spacer to the adjoining wall, making sure not to turn the tile that is being marked. Make a second mark on the tile as in step 1. Cut the tile and install.

How to Cut Square Notches

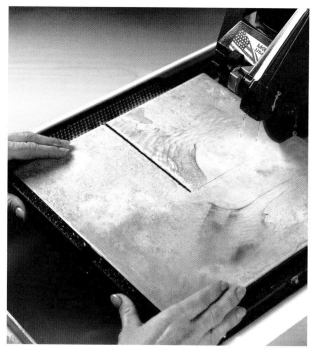

Cut along the marked line on one side of the notch. Turn the tile and cut along the other line to complete the notch. To keep the tile from breaking before you're through, slow down as you get close to the intersection with the first cut.

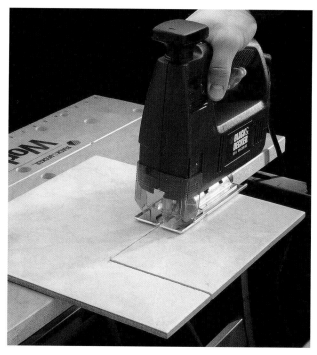

To cut square notches in a small number of wall tiles, clamp the tile down on a worktable, then use a jigsaw with a tungsten carbide blade to make the cuts. If you need to notch quite a few tiles, a wet saw is more efficient.

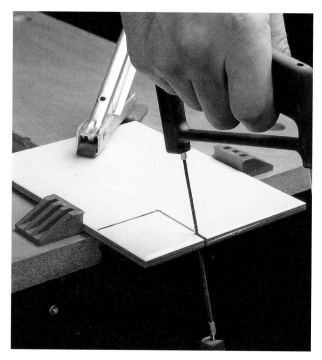

To make a small number of cuts in wall tile, you can use a rod saw. Fit a tungsten carbide rod saw into a hacksaw body. Firmly support the tile and use a sawing motion to cut the tile.

To make a very small notch, use tile nippers. Score the lines and then nibble up to the lines, biting very small pieces at a time.

How to Mark & Cut Irregular Notches

Make a paper template of the contour or use a contour gauge. To use a contour gauge, press the gauge onto the profile and trace it onto the tile.

Use a wet saw to make a series of closely spaced, parallel cuts, then nip away the waste.

How to Make Curved Cuts

Mark a cutting line on the tile face, then use the scoring wheel of a hand-held tile cutter to score the cut line. Make several parallel scores, no more than ¼" apart, in the waste portion of the tile.

Use tile nippers to nibble away the scored portion of the tile.

How to Mark & Cut Holes in Tile

1

Align the tile to be cut with the last full row of tile and butt it against the pipe. Mark the center of the pipe onto the front edge of the tile.

2

Place a ¼" spacer against the wall and butt the tile against it. Mark the pipe center on the side edge of the tile. Using a combination square, draw a line through each mark to the edges of the tile.

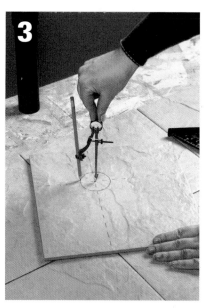

3

Starting from the intersection of the lines at the center, draw a circle slightly larger than the pipe or protrusion.

4

Drill around the edges of the hole, using a ceramic tile bit. Gently knock out the waste material with a hammer. The rough edges of the hole will be covered by a protective plate (called an escutcheon).

Variation: Score and cut the tile so the hole is divided in half, using the straight-cut method (page 6), then use the curved-cut method (page 9) to remove waste material from each half of the circle.

How to Drill Holes in Tile

1

Make a dimple with a center punch to break through the glaze, to keep the drill bit from wandering.

2

Select a tungsten carbide hole saw in the appropriate size and attach it to a power drill. Place the tip at the marked center and drill the hole.

Making Specialty Cuts ▶

Score cuts on mosaic tiles with a tile cutter in the row where the cut will occur. Cut away excess strips of mosaics from the sheet, using a utility knife, then use a handheld tile cutter to snap tiles one at a time. *Note: Use tile nippers to cut narrow portions of tiles after scoring.*

3. Mixing & Using Mortar

Thinset mortar is a fine-grained cement product used to adhere underlayment to the subfloor and to bond ceramic tile to underlayment. Some mortars include a latex additive in the dry mix, but with others, you'll need to add liquid latex additive as you prepare the mortar.

When mixing mortar, start with the dry powder and gradually add water, stirring the mixture to achieve a creamy consistency. You want the mortar wet enough for the tiles to stick, but not so wet that it's runny. Once the mortar is spread on the floor or wall, the ridges of the mortar should hold their shape.

Mortar is spread on the underlayment or substrate with a notched trowel. The edge of the trowel creates furrows in the mortar bed, then tile is placed on the mortar using a twisting motion.

As you install tiles, spread only as much mortar as you can use in 10 minutes. If the mortar sits too long, it will begin to harden and the tiles will not adhere to it. If it does begin to harden, scrape it up, throw it away, and spread new mortar.

How to Mix Mortar

To prepare small batches (above), add liquid, a little at a time, to the dry powder and stir the mixture until it has a creamy consistency. If you're adding liquid latex additive, mix it in when the mixture nears the proper consistency.

To prepare large batches or a series of batches (above), use a ½" drill and a mortar mixing paddle. This job easily can burn out a standard ⅜" drill, so it's worth the money to rent a heavy-duty drill if you don't have one.

Options for Mortaring Tile

Spread mortar evenly onto the floor, using the appropriate trowel. Use the notched edge of the trowel to create furrows in the mortar bed.

Butter individual tiles by applying thinset mortar directly to the back of the tile. Use the notched edge of the trowel to furrow the mortar.

Butter each wall tile and apply it to the wall with a slight twisting motion.

Variation: Spread the mortar on a small section of wall, then set the tiles into it. Thinset mortar sets quickly, so work quickly if you choose this method.

4. Tools for Cutting Tile

Even though tile is a rigid material, it can be cut to fit a variety of applications. With the proper tools, tile can be trimmed, notched, and drilled. If you're planning only one tile project, consider renting the more expensive pieces of equipment.

Coping saws with rod saw blades are usually adequate for cutting soft tile, such as wall tile.

Tile nippers are used to create curves and circles. Tile is first marked with the scoring wheel of a hand-held tile cutter or a wet saw blade to create a cutting guide.

Hand-held tile cutters are used to snap tiles one at a time. They are often used for cutting mosaic tiles after they have been scored.

Tile stones file away rough edges left by tile nippers and hand-held tile cutters. Stones can also be used to shave off small amounts of tile for fitting.

Wet saws, also called "tile saws," employ water to cool both the blade and the tile during cutting. This tool is used primarily for cutting floor tile—especially natural stone tile—but it is also useful for quickly cutting large quantities of tile or notches in hard tile.

Diamond blades are used on hand-held wet saws and grinders to cut through the hardest tile materials such as pavers, marble, granite, slate, and other natural stone.

Tile cutters are quick, efficient tools for scoring and cutting straight lines in most types of light- to medium-weight tile.

Grinders come in handy for cutting granite and marble when equipped with a diamond blade. Cuts made with this hand tool will be less accurate than with a wet saw, so it is best used to cut tile for areas that will be covered with molding or fixtures.

Coping saw with rod saw blade

Tile nippers

Hand-held tile cutter

Tile stone

Wet saw

Diamond blade

Tile cutter

Grinder

5. Tools for Setting & Grouting Tile

Laying tile requires quick, precise work, so it's wise to assemble the necessary supplies before you begin. You don't want to search for a tool with wet mortar already in place. Most of the tools required for setting and grouting tile are probably already in your tool box, so take an inventory before you head to the home center or hardware store.

Tile spacers are essential for achieving consistent spacing between tiles. They are set at corners of laid tile and are later removed so grout can be applied.

Grout sponges, buff rags, foam brushes, and grout sealer applicators are used after grout is applied. Grout sponges are used to wipe away grout residue, buff rags remove grout haze, and foam brushes and grout sealer applicators are for applying grout sealer.

Rubber mallets are used to gently tap tiles and set them evenly into mortar.

Needlenose pliers come in handy for removing spacers placed between tiles.

Caulk guns are used to fill expansion joints at the floor and base trim, at inside corners, and where tile meets surfaces made of other materials.

Grout floats are used to apply grout over tile and into joints. They are also used to remove excess grout from the surface of tiles after grout has been applied. For mosaic sheets, grout floats are handy for gently pressing tile into mortar.

Trowels are used to apply mortar to surfaces where tile will be laid and to apply mortar directly to the backs of cut tiles.

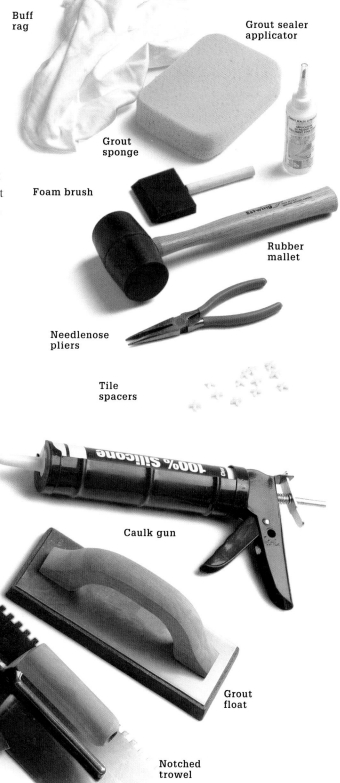

Buff rag

Grout sealer applicator

Grout sponge

Foam brush

Rubber mallet

Needlenose pliers

Tile spacers

Caulk gun

Trowel

Grout float

Notched trowel

6. Preparation Materials

The type of substrate you lay for ceramic tile will depend on where your new surface will be. Where moisture will be present, cementboard or fiber/cementboard should be installed. In other areas, plywood or cork can be suitable. Over concrete, isolation membrane may be required. Installing the proper foundation for your project will help prevent cracks and deterioration in laid tile.

Cork makes an excellent underlayment when sound control and warmth are an issue. In areas where moisture may be present, a waterproof membrane or sealant should be applied first.

Fiber/cementboard is a thin, high-density underlayment used in wet areas where floor height is a concern.

Cementboard remains stable even when exposed to moisture, so it is a good choice for wet tile areas, such as bathrooms.

Greenboard is drywall treated to withstand occasional moisture. It is a good choice for walls in bathrooms and other humid areas.

Plywood is a good, all-around underlayment in low-moisture areas. For ceramic tile installations, use ½" exterior-grade AC plywood.

Trowel-applied membrane is a paste form of water-proofing membrane that can be applied in areas that will be exposed to moisture.

Mesh tape or fiberglass tape is applied to cementboard seams, then a thin layer of mortar is applied over the tape to seal them.

Waterproofing membrane is applied over existing flooring and non-water-resistant substrate in areas that will be exposed to moisture.

Shower pan liners are used to create custom shower pans.

Isolation membrane is used either in strips or as a floor underlayment to cover cracks in concrete floors and protect tiles from movement.

Trowel-applied membrane

Waterproofing membrane

Fiberglass tape

Shower pan liner

Isolation membrane

Plywood

Greenboard

Cementboard

Fiber/cementboard

Cork

7. Materials for Setting & Grouting Tile

To ensure your tiling project lasts, it's important to set and grout the tile properly. Follow directions for mixing and applying mortars, fortifiers, and adhesives. Then seal grout to keep your tile beautiful and long-lasting.

Thinset mortar is a cement-based adhesive that is purchased in dry form and prepared by adding liquid until a creamy consistency is achieved. Some mortars include a latex additive in the dry mix. Other mortars require a liquid latex additive.

Grout fills the spaces between tiles and is available in pre-tinted colors to match your tile. Grout width should be considered a decorative element of your tile project.

Latex fortifier is a liquid added to mortar to strengthen its bonding power. Some mortar powders include fortifier in the dry mix.

Grout sealer is applied with a sponge brush to ward off stains and make tile maintenance easier.

Wall tile mastic is used to install base-trim tile.

Wall and floor tile adhesive is available in pre-mixed formulas. Thinset mortar is, however, recommended for most flooring installations.

Thinset mortar

Grout

Latex fortifier

Wall tile mastic

Grout sealer

Floor tile adhesive

8. Installing Underlayment

Ceramic and natural stone tile floors often require an underlayment that stands up to moisture, such as cementboard. If you will use your old flooring as underlayment, apply an embossing leveler to prepare it for the new installation (see below, right).

When installing new underlayment, make sure it is securely attached to the subfloor in all areas, including below all movable appliances. Notch the underlayment to fit room contours. Around door casings and other moldings, undercut the moldings and insert the underlayment beneath them.

Plywood is typically used as an underlayment for vinyl flooring and for ceramic tile installations in dry areas. For ceramic tile, use ½" exterior-grade AC plywood. Do not use particleboard, oriented-strand board, or treated lumber as underlayment for tile.

Fiber/cementboard is a thin, high-density underlayment used under ceramic tile in situations where floor height is a concern. (For installation, follow the steps for cementboard, on page 24.)

Cementboard is used exclusively for ceramic or stone tile installations. It remains stable even when exposed to moisture and is therefore the best underlayment to use in areas likely to get wet, such as bathrooms.

Isolation membrane is used to protect ceramic tile installations from movement that may occur on cracked concrete floors. It is often used to cover individual cracks, but it can also be used over an entire floor. Isolation membrane is also available in a liquid form that can be poured over the project area.

Plywood

Fiber/cementboard

Cementboard

Isolation membrane

Tool Tip ▸

Embossing leveler is a mortar-like substance used for preparing well-adhered resilient flooring or ceramic tile for use as an underlayment. Mix the leveler according to the manufacturer's directions, and spread it thinly over the floor with a flat-edged trowel. Wipe away any excess, making sure all dips and indentations are filled. Work quickly—embossing leveler begins to set in 10 minutes. After the leveler dries, scrape away ridges and high spots with the trowel.

Tools & Materials ▸

Drill	Plywood underlayment
Circular saw	1" deck screws
Wallboard knife	Floor-patching
Power sander	compound
¼" notched trowel	Latex additive
Straightedge	Thinset mortar
Utility knife	1½" galvanized deck
Jigsaw with carbide	screws
blade	Cementboard
⅛" notched trowel	Fiberglass-mesh
Flooring roller	wallboard tape

How to Install Plywood Underlayment

1

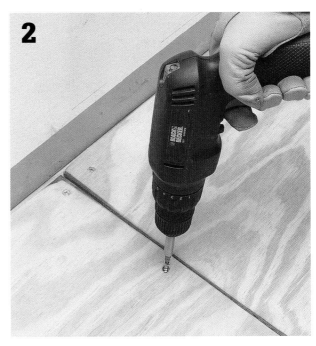

2

Begin by installing a full sheet of plywood along the longest wall, making sure the underlayment seams will not be aligned with the subfloor seams. Fasten the plywood to the subfloor, using 1" deck screws driven every 6" along the edges and at 8" intervals in the field of the sheet.

Continue fastening sheets of plywood to the subfloor, driving the screw heads slightly below the underlayment surface. Leave ¼" expansion gaps at the walls and between sheets. Offset seams in subsequent rows.

3

4

5

Using a circular saw or jigsaw, notch plywood to meet existing flooring in doorways, then fasten the notched sheets to the subfloor.

Mix floor-patching compound and latex or acrylic additive, according to the manufacturer's directions. Spread it over seams and screw heads with a wallboard knife.

Let the patching compound dry, then sand the patched areas, using a power sander.

How to Install Cementboard

1

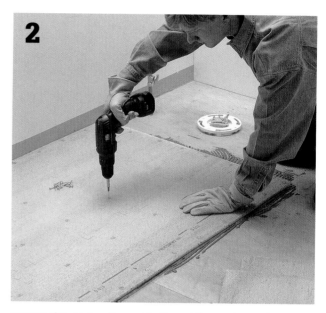

2

Mix thinset mortar (see page 12) according to the manufacturer's directions. Starting at the longest wall, spread the mortar on the subfloor in a figure-eight pattern, using a ¼" notched trowel. Spread only enough mortar for one sheet at a time. Set the cementboard on the mortar with the rough side up, making sure the edges are offset from the subfloor seams.

Fasten the cementboard to the subfloor, using 1½" galvanized deck screws driven every 6" along edges and 8" throughout the sheet. Drive the screw heads flush with the surface. Continue spreading mortar and installing sheets along the wall.

3

4

5

Cut cementboard pieces as necessary, leaving a ⅛" gap at all joints and a ¼" gap along the room perimeter. For straight cuts, use a utility knife to score a line through the fiber-mesh layer just beneath the surface, then snap the board along the scored line.

To cut holes, notches, or irregular shapes, use a jigsaw with a carbide blade. Continue installing cementboard sheets to cover the entire floor. Inset: A flange extender or additional wax ring may be needed to ensure a proper toilet installation after additional layers of underlayment have been installed in a bathroom.

Place fiberglass-mesh wallboard tape over the seams. Use a wallboard knife to apply thinset mortar to the seams, filling the gaps between sheets and spreading a thin layer of mortar over the tape. Allow the mortar to cure for two days before starting the tile installation.

How to Install Isolation Membrane

Thoroughly clean the subfloor, then apply thinset mortar (see page 12) with a ⅛" notched trowel. Start spreading the mortar along a wall in a section as wide as the membrane and 8 to 10 ft. long. *Note: For some membranes, you must use a bonding material other than mortar. Read and follow label directions.*

Roll out the membrane over the mortar. Cut the membrane to fit tightly against the walls, using a straightedge and utility knife.

Starting in the center of the membrane, use a heavy flooring roller (available at rental centers) to smooth out the surface toward the edges. This frees trapped air and presses out excess bonding material.

Repeat steps 1 through 3, cutting the membrane as necessary at the walls and obstacles, until the floor is completely covered with membrane. Do not overlap the seams, but make sure they are tight. Allow the mortar to cure for two days before installing the tile.

9. Installing & Finishing Wallboard

Regular wallboard is an appropriate backer for ceramic tile in dry locations. Greenboard, a moisture-resistent form of wallboard, is good for kitchens and the dry areas of bathrooms. Tub and shower surrounds and kitchen backsplashes should have a cementboard backer.

Wallboard panels are available in 4 × 8-ft. or 4 × 10-ft. sheets, and in ⅜", ½", and ⅝" thicknesses. For new walls, ½" thick is standard.

Install wallboard panels so that seams fall over the center of framing members, not at sides. Use all-purpose wallboard compound and paper joint tape to finish seams.

Tools & Materials ▸

Tape measure
Utility knife
Wallboard
T-square
6" and 12"
   wallboard knives
150-grit sanding
   sponge

Screw gun
Wallboard
Wallboard tape
1¼" coarse-thread
   wallboard screws
Wallboard compound
Metal inside corner bead
Taping knife

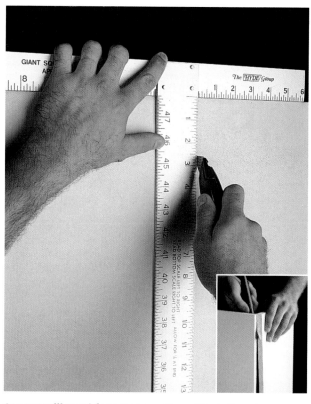

Score wallboard face paper with a utility knife, using a drywall T-square as a guide. Bend the panel away from the scored line until the core breaks, then cut through the back paper (inset) with a utility knife, and separate the pieces.

How to Install and Finish Wallboard

Install panels with their tapered edges butted together. Fasten with 1¼" wallboard screws, driven every 8" along the edges, and every 12" in the field. Drive screws deep enough to dimple surface without ripping face paper (inset).

Finish the seams by applying an even bed layer of wallboard compound over the seam, about ⅛" thick, using a 6" taping knife.

Center the wallboard tape over the seam and lightly embed it into the compound, making sure it's smooth and straight.

4

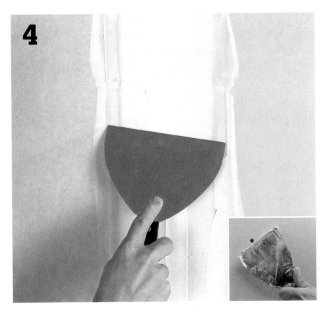

Smooth the tape with the taping knife. Apply enough pressure to force compound from underneath the tape, leaving the tape flat and with a thin layer underneath. Cover all exposed screw heads with the first of three coats of compound (inset). Let compound dry overnight.

5

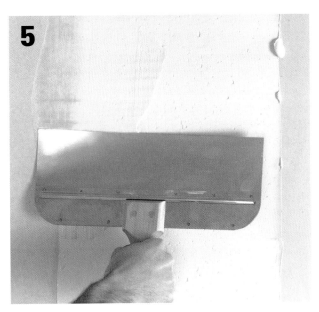

Second-coat the seams with a thin, even layer of compound, using a 12" knife. Feather the sides of the compound first, holding the blade almost flat and applying pressure to the outside of the blade so the blade just skims over the center of the seam.

6

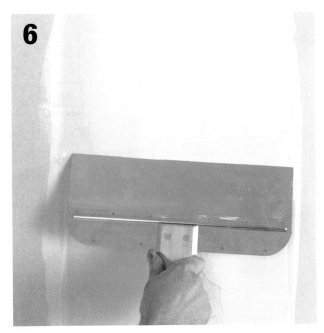

After feathering both sides, make a pass down the center of the seam, leaving the seam smooth and even, the edges feathered out even with the wallboard surface. Completely cover the joint tape. Let the second coat dry, then apply a third coat, using the 12" knife. After the third coat dries completely, sand the compound lightly with a wallboard sander or a 150-grit sanding sponge.

Tool Tip ▸

Finish any inside corners, using paper-faced metal inside corner bead to produce straight, durable corners with little fuss. Embed the bead into a thin layer of compound, then smooth the paper with a taping knife. Apply two finish coats to the corner, then sand the compound smooth.

10. Installing Cementboard

Use tile backer board as the substrate for tile walls in wet areas. Unlike wallboard, tile backer won't break down and cause damage if water gets behind the tile. The three basic types of tile backer are cementboard, fiber-cement board, and Dens-Shield.

Though water cannot damage either cementboard or fiber-cement board, it can pass through them. To protect the framing members, install a water barrier of 4-mil plastic or 15# building paper behind the backer.

Dens-Shield has a waterproof acrylic facing that provides the water barrier. It cuts and installs much like wallboard, but it requires galvanized screws to prevent corrosion and must be sealed with caulk at all untaped joints and penetrations.

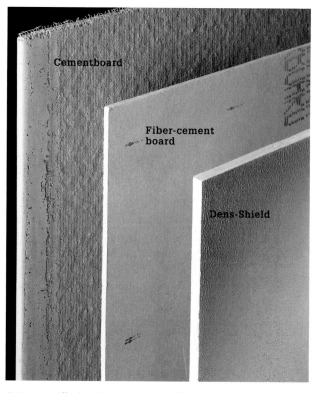

Common tile backers are cementboard, fiber-cementboard, and Dens-Shield. Cementboard is made from portland cement and sand reinforced by an outer layer of fiberglass mesh. Fiber-cement board is made similarly, but with a fiber reinforcement integrated throughout the panel. Dens-Shield is a water-resistant gypsum board with a waterproof acrylic facing.

Tools & Materials ▸

Utility knife	Stapler
T-square	Drill
Drill with a small	4-mil plastic sheeting
masonry bit	Cementboard
Hammer	1¼" cementboard screws
Jigsaw with a	Cementboard joint tape
bimetal blade	Latex-portland cement
Wallboard knife	mortar
Carbide-tipped	15# building paper
cutter	

How to Install Cementboard

Staple a water barrier of 4-mil plastic sheeting or 15# building paper over the framing. Overlap seams by several inches, and leave the sheets long at the perimeter. *Note: Framing for cementboard must be 16" on-center; steel studs must be 20-gauge.*

Cut cementboard by scoring through the mesh just below the surface, using a utility knife or carbide-tipped cutter. Snap the panel back, then cut through the back-side mesh (inset). *Note: For tile applications, the rough face of the board is the front.*

Make cutouts for pipes and other penetrations by drilling a series of holes through the board, using a small masonry bit. Tap the hole out with a hammer or a scrap of pipe. Cut holes along edges with a jigsaw and bimetal blade.

4

Install the sheets horizontally. Where possible, use full pieces to avoid cut-and-butted seams, which are difficult to fasten. If there are vertical seams, stagger them between rows. Leave a ⅛" gap between sheets at vertical seams and corners. Use spacers to set the bottom row of panels ¼" above the tub or shower base. Fasten the sheets with 1¼" cementboard screws, driven every 8" for walls and every 6" for ceilings. Drive the screws ½" from the edges to prevent crumbling. If the studs are steel, don't fasten within 1" of the top track.

5

Cover the joints and corners with cementboard joint tape (alkali-resistant fiberglass mesh) and latex-portland cement mortar (thinset). Apply a layer of mortar with a wallboard knife, embed the tape into the mortar, then smooth and level the mortar.

Variation: Finishing Cementboard ▸

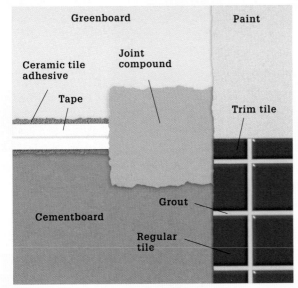

Greenboard · Paint

Ceramic tile adhesive

Joint compound

Tape

Trim tile

Grout

Cementboard

Regular tile

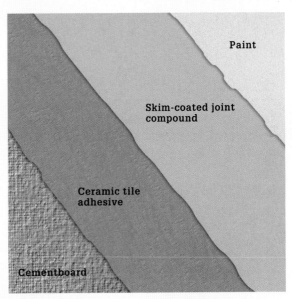

Paint

Skim-coated joint compound

Ceramic tile adhesive

Cementboard

To finish a joint between cementboard and greenboard, seal the joint and exposed cementboard with ceramic tile adhesive, a mixture of four parts adhesive to one part water. Embed paper joint tape into the adhesive, smoothing the tape with a tape knife. Allow the adhesive to dry, then finish the joint with at least two coats of all-purpose wallboard joint compound.

To finish small areas of cementboard that will not be tiled, seal the cementboard with ceramic tile adhesive, a mixture of four parts adhesive to one part water, then apply a skim-coat of all-purpose wallboard joint compound, using a 12" wallboard knife. Then paint the wall.

11. Installing Wall Membranes

Wall membranes may provide waterproofing or isolation from small underlayment movement, or both. Because water does not sit on wall surfaces as it does on floors, waterproofing of walls is not as critical. In most cases, plastic sheeting or building paper behind cement backer board is sufficient. Saunas and steam rooms may need additional waterproofing.

Isolation membrane comes in roll- or trowel-on forms as well as in sheet form. It can be applied to existing cracks or potential areas of movement. Check the product directions for the maximum width crack or expansion joint that can be spanned and the type of substrate on which it can be used.

It is important to apply isolation membrane to concrete walls to prevent hairline cracks from being transferred outward to the tile or grout surface. Some products combine waterproofing and isolation properties. The tile adhesive is applied directly to the isolation membrane after it has cured.

Be sure to check for compatibility between the roll- or trowel-on membranes and your particular application needs. Fountains and pools have specific waterproofing needs—check with your tile dealer if you plan on using wall tile for a pool wall.

Plastic sheeting, sheet membrane, building paper, and trowel-applied membrane are all options for adding waterproofing to walls. Isolation membranes in strips or sheets also protect tile surfaces from cracking caused by small movements in the underlayment.

A water barrier of 4-mil plastic sheeting can be stapled to studs before installing cementboard or fiber-cement board.

Building paper (15#) can also be used as a water barrier behind cementboard and fiber-cement board. Start from the bottom and install horizontally so each layer overlaps the previous one by two inches.

Waterproofing/isolation membranes are an easy way to add waterproofing and crack protection to existing walls. This application is especially suited to smooth, solid concrete surfaces. The tile adhesive is applied directly to the membrane after it dries.

Isolation membrane may be used on wall and ceiling surfaces in areas such as steam rooms and saunas that have extreme temperature fluctuation and high humidity. The membrane is typically installed with mortar, but some membranes must be used with a specific bonding agent.

12. Laying Out Floor Designs

Once you have a stable, firm, smooth substrate in place, the next step is laying out the project. While it might be tempting to go directly to laying the tile, resist the temptation. Planning is a very important step in the process and one that pays off in the long run. There are few things more frustrating than running into issues that could have been avoided through a little more attention to detail on the front end.

A tile floor essentially is a giant grid, and imperfections can be quite obvious, especially if the grout contrasts sharply with the tile.

Good layouts start with accurate measurements and detailed scale drawings. Use these drawings to experiment with potential layouts until you're satisfied. Try to:

- Center the tile within the room and keep the final tiles at opposite sides equal in size.
- Minimize the number of cuts required.
- Disguise disparities in rooms that are not square.

Laying out borders, diagonal sets, or running bonds involves a few special considerations that are also discussed in the following pages.

Drawing Layouts for Floor Designs

It's not necessary to draw layouts for projects in small, square rooms with no tricky issues. On the other hand, drawings are helpful for projects in rooms that have more than four corners or are more than an inch out of square, and for projects that involve several adjacent rooms.

To start, measure the room. Figure out a scale that's easy to use—one square per tile for larger-scale graph paper or four squares per tile on smaller-scale graph paper—and draw the room. Make several copies of the drawing so you can experiment with layouts without redoing it.

Next, lay out at least 10 tiles with spacers and measure them. Add the thickness of one grout line and divide the total by 10 to calculate the exact size of one tile with grout. Using this calculation and the same scale as you used for the room diagram, draw layouts until you find one that works. Sometimes there's no way to avoid narrow tiles at the edges. In that case, plan to put them along the least visible wall in the room or in areas that will be covered with furniture or fixtures.

Confirm your calculations by testing the layout. No matter how careful you are, it's possible to make mistakes when you're working with drawings and measurements. It's much better to discover any miscalculations before setting any tile or spreading any mortar. Lay out one complete row of full-sized tile in at least two directions. Adjust the layout as necessary.

If the layout is complicated or involves lots of cuts, it's worth the time to dry-fit the entire floor.

How to Test Corners for Square

To get accurate room measurements, start in a corner of the room and measure along the wall to the opposite corner. Do this for each wall, writing down the measurements as you go. When measuring to locate permanent obstacles or fixtures, pick a point and take all measurements from it. That way you'll have a constant reference point when you diagram the room.

Check for square by measuring a corner. On one wall, mark a spot 3 feet from the corner; on the other wall, mark a spot 4 feet from the corner. Measure between the marks. If the distance between the marks is exactly 5 feet, the room is square. For greater accuracy in larger rooms, use multiples of 3, 4, and 5 such as 6, 8, and 10, or 9, 12, and 15.

How to Lay Out Floor Designs

Diagram the entire room, drawing it to scale including any permanent fixtures such as cabinets and stairways. Draw possible tile layouts, at the same scale as your room drawing, on transparency paper and place them over the room diagram. Experiment with layouts until you find a successful arrangement.

Make a story stick to help you estimate how many tiles will fit in a given area. Lay out a row of tile, with spacers, and set an 8-ft.-long 1 × 2 next to it. (Position the end of the 1 × 2 in the center of a grout line.) Holding the board in place, mark the edges of each grout line.

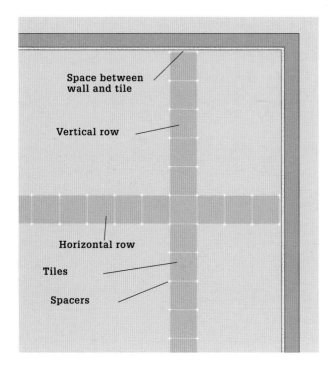

Space between wall and tile

Vertical row

Horizontal row

Tiles

Spacers

Test the layout by setting out one vertical and one horizontal row of tile, all the way to the walls in both directions.

Dry-lay the tile if you're working with a complex layout, tiling around a series of obstacles, or setting tiles on the diagonal. You may find that you need to shift the layout slightly to keep from cutting very small tile for edges or corners.

Establishing Reference Lines for Floor Designs

Reference lines are used as guides for the first tiles laid. Before you snap these lines, think about where to start tiling. The goal is to work it out so that you don't need to step on recently laid tile in order to continue working. It often makes sense to start in the middle of a room, but not always—sometimes it's better to start a few feet from a wall and work your way across the room. If a room has only one door, start at the far end and move toward the door. Give some thought to the issue and make sure you don't tile yourself into a corner!

Another way to help keep the tile straight is by using a batten, which is nothing more than a long, straight board used as a guide. A piece of plywood works well if you maintain the factory edge. Just position the board and tack it in place, using several screws. Butt the first row of tile up to it and leave it in place until the mortar starts to dry. Remove the batten and continue setting tile. Maintaining even spacing will maintain the straight lines.

How to Mark Reference Lines for Straight Sets

Position a reference line (X) by measuring between opposite sides of the room and marking the center of each side. Snap a chalk line between these marks.

Measure and mark the centerpoint of the chalk line. From this point, use a framing square to establish a second line perpendicular to the first. Snap a second reference line (Y) across the room.

How to Mark Reference Lines for Diagonal Sets

Snap reference lines that meet in the exact center of the room. Make sure the lines are perpendicular, then mark a point on each line precisely the same distance from the center.

Snap lines to connect the marked points. The sides of the resulting square will be tilted at a 45° angle to the room. Use the square to create working lines for laying out the room.

How to Mark Reference Lines for Running Bond Sets

Snap perpendicular reference lines as described on page 31. Dry-fit a few tiles side by side, using spacers. Offset the rows by a measurement that's equal to one-half the length of the tile and one-half the width of the grout line. Measure the total width of the dry-fitted section.

Use this measurement to snap a series of equally spaced parallel lines to help keep your tiles straight during installation. (Running-bond layouts are most effective with rectangular tiles.)

Planning Borders & Design Areas

A border can divide a floor into sections or it can define a design area such as the one shown at right. You can create a design inside the border by merely turning the tiles at a 45° angle, by installing decorative tiles, or by creating a mosaic. Such designs should cover between 25 and 50 percent of the floor. If the design is too small, it'll get lost in the floor. If it's too big, it'll be distracting.

Determine the size and location of the border on graph paper, then transfer those measurements onto the floor. A dry run with the border and field tile is essential.

The tile is installed in three stages. The border is placed first, followed by outside field tile, then the tile within the border.

How to Lay Out a Border

1

Measure the length and width of the room in which you'll be installing the border.

2

Transfer the measurements onto paper by making a scale drawing of the room. Include the locations of cabinets, doors, permanent fixtures, and furniture.

3

Determine the size of the border you want. Bordered designs should be between ¼ and ½ the area of the room. Draw the border on transparency paper, using the same scale as the room drawing.

4

Place the transparency of the border over the room drawing. Move it around to find the best layout. Tape the border transparency in place over the room drawing. Draw perpendicular lines through the center of the border and calculate the distance from the center lines to the border.

5

Transfer the measurements from the border transparency onto your floor, starting with your center lines. Snap chalk lines to establish your layout for the border.

6

Lay out the border along the reference lines in a dry run. Do a dry run of the field tiles inside and outside of the border along the center lines. Make any adjustments, if necessary.

13. Laying Out Wall Designs

Wall projects can be challenging because walls are so rarely plumb and true. In some cases, that means the walls themselves need to be adjusted before the tile portion of the project begins. Most of the time, though, it simply means being aware of the issues and working around them as discussed in the following pages. (If your walls need work before you begin tiling them, consult pages 22 to 27 for ideas and information.)

Layout is critical to successful wall projects. Start with accurate measurements and draw the room to scale.

Use the drawing to experiment with potential arrangements. The goal is to arrive at a layout that gives the walls a balanced, symmetrical look.

- Center the tile within the room and keep the final tiles at opposite sides equal in size.
- Minimize the number of cuts required and avoid cutting very narrow pieces of tile.
- Disguise disparities on walls that are not square.
- Plan effective placement of borders, liners, and trim.

Drawing Layouts for Wall Designs

It may not be necessary to draw layouts for small, simple projects, but it's a good idea if you're tiling more than one wall, creating designs or borders, or working with walls that aren't plumb or a room that's out of square by more than an inch. Start by checking to see whether the walls are plumb. Place a carpenter's level along the edge of a straight board, then place the board against the walls and on the floor at the bottom of the walls. If a wall is out of square by more than ¼" per 8 feet, you'll need to add moldings, build up the wall with joint compound, or trim the tiles in a way that makes the imperfection less obvious. Check outside corners for plumb and make careful note of any problems.

Now, measure and draw the walls on graph paper, including windows, doors, and permanent fixtures such as bathtubs. (Figure out a scale that's easy to use—one square per tile for larger-scale graph paper or four squares per tile on smaller-scale graph paper.) Make several copies of the drawing so you can experiment with layouts without redrawing it.

Double check the size of your tile, including borders or accent tiles, and begin evaluating layouts. The goal is to make the room look balanced and to place cut tile in the least visible positions. For example, if the height of a wall above a sink or bathtub can't be covered in full tile, it's best to put cut tile on the bottom row so that the top row (which is more visible) is composed of full tile. If you're adding accents, position them so that the repeating pattern is even or at least balanced across the wall.

How to Draw a Tile Layout for Wall Designs

1

Check the walls and corners to see if they're plumb. Make any adjustments necessary before beginning your tile project.

2

Measure the walls, paying particular attention to the placement of windows, doors, and permanent fixtures. Use these measurements to create a scale drawing of each wall to be tiled.

Lay out your tiles, accents, and trim. Take measurements of the tile layout.

Draw your tile layout to scale on the wall drawing to establish your reference lines.

Testing Wall Layouts

Establishing perpendicular reference lines is a critical part of every tile project, including wall projects. To create these lines, measure and mark the midpoint at the top and bottom of the wall, and then again along each side. Snap chalk lines between opposite marks to create your vertical and horizontal centerlines. Use the 3-4-5 triangle method to make sure the lines are drawn correctly (see page 29). Adjust the lines until they are exactly perpendicular.

Next, do a dry run of your proposed layout, starting at the center of the wall and working toward an adjoining wall. If the gap between the last full tile and the wall is too narrow, adjust your starting point. Continue to dry-fit tile along the walls, paying special attention to any windows, doors, or permanent fixtures in the wall. If you end up with very narrow tiles anywhere, adjust the reference lines (and your layout) to avoid them. It's best not to cut tiles by more than half.

If your wall has an outside corner, start your dry run there. Place bullnose tiles over the edges of the adjoining field tiles. If this results in a narrow gap at the opposite wall, install trimmed tile next to the bullnose edge to even out or avoid the gap.

Measure and mark the horizontal and vertical midpoints of the wall, then snap chalk lines between sets of opposite marks. Use the 3-4-5 triangle method (see page 29) to make sure the lines are perpendicular to one another.

How to Test a Wall Layout

Attach a batten to the wall along your horizontal reference line, using screws. Dry-fit tiles on the batten, aligning the middle tile with the vertical centerline.

If you end up with too narrow a gap along the wall in step 1, move over half the width of a tile by centering the middle tile over the vertical centerline.

Use a story stick (see page 30) to determine whether your planned layout works vertically. If necessary, adjust the size of the first row of tile.

Dry-fit the first row of tile, then hold a story stick along the horizontal guideline with one grout line matched to the vertical reference line. Mark the grout lines, which will correspond with the grout lines of the first row and can be used as reference points.

How to Work Around Outside Corners

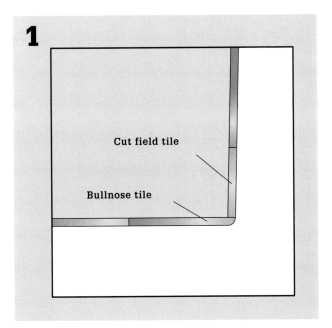

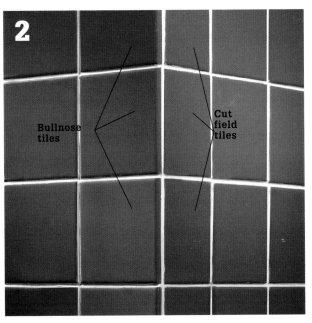

Overlap field tiles with bullnose tiles on outside corners. Try to use whole tiles on the corner, but if that's not possible, plan to trim the field tiles. If the wall is slightly out of plumb and not very wide, line up the bullnose tiles so they overlap the field tiles evenly.

Disguise walls that are badly out of plumb by installing the field tile on that side, trimming them as necessary. Overlap the cut edges with bullnose tiles. Install tiles on both walls at the same time, making sure the bullnose pieces cover the cut edges.

How to Work Around Windows

Use a story stick to evaluate the layout around obstacles, such as windows. Adjust reference lines as necessary to avoid cutting tiles by more than half, either vertically or horizontally.

Remove aprons (on windows that have them) and tile up to the window, then replace the trim. Aprons are the only window trim that can be removed and replaced in this manner.

14. Installing a Tile Floor

Tile flooring should be durable and slip-resistant. Look for floor tile that is textured or soft-glazed—for slip resistance—and has a Class or Group rating of 3, 4, or 5—for strength. Floor tile should also be glazed for protection from staining. If you use unglazed tile, be sure to seal it properly after installation. See pages 11 through 35 for more information on selecting floor tile.

Standard grouts also need stain protection. Mix your grout with a latex additive, and apply a grout sealer after the new grout sets, then reapply the sealer once a year thereafter. Successful tile installation involves careful preparation of the floor and the proper combination of materials. For an underlayment, cementboard is the best for use over wood subfloors in bathrooms, since it is stable and undamaged by moisture (page 24). Thinset is the most common adhesive for floor tile. It comes as a dry powder that is mixed with water. Premixed organic adhesives generally are not recommended for floors.

If you want to install trim tiles, consider their placement as you plan the layout. Some base-trim tile is set on the floor, with its finished edge flush with the field tile; other types are installed on top of the field tile.

Tools & Materials ▸

Chalk line	Foam brush
¼" square-notched trowel	Tile
	Thinset mortar
Drill	Tile spacers
Rubber mallet	2 × 4
Tile-cutting tools	Threshold material
Needlenose pliers	Grout
Utility knife	Latex additive
Grout float	(mortar and grout)
Grout sponge	Grout sealer
Buff rag	Silicone caulk

Trim and finishing materials for tile installations include base-trim tiles (A), which fit around the room perimeter, and bullnose tiles (B), used at doorways and other transition areas. Doorway thresholds (C) are made from synthetic materials as well as natural materials, such as marble, and come in thicknesses ranging from ¼" to ¾" to match different floor levels.

How to Install Cementboard Underlayment

1

Starting at the longest wall, spread thinset mortar on the subfloor in a figure-eight pattern. Spread only enough mortar for one sheet at a time. (See pages 12 to 13 for a full description of how to mix and apply thinset mortar.) Set the cementboard on the mortar with the rough side up, making sure the edges are offset from the subfloor seams.

2

Fasten cementboard to the subfloor, using 1½" cementboard screws. Drive the screw heads flush with the surface. Continue spreading mortar and installing sheets along the wall, leaving a ⅛" gap at all joints and a ¼" gap along the room perimeter. (See page 24 for full description of installing cementboard).

Establishing Reference Lines for Floor Tile Installation ▸

To establish reference lines, position the first line (X) between the centerpoints of opposite sides of the room. Snap a chalk line between these points. Next, establish a second line perpendicular to the first. Snap a second reference line (Y) across the room.

Make sure the lines are exactly perpendicular, using the 3-4-5 triangle method. (For a full description of establishing perpendicular reference lines for floor projects, see page 31).

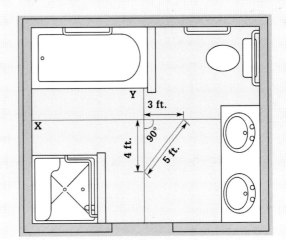

How to Install a Tile Floor

Draw reference lines and dry-fit full tiles along both lines, adjusting the layout as necessary. Mix a batch of thinset mortar (see pages 12 to 13), and spread it evenly against both reference lines of one quadrant. Use the notched edge of the trowel to create furrows in the mortar bed. *Note: For large or uneven tiles, you may need a trowel with ⅜" or larger notches.*

Set the first tile in the corner of the quadrant where the reference lines intersect. When setting tiles that are 8" square or larger, twist each tile slightly as you set it into position.

Using a soft rubber mallet, gently rap the central area of each tile a few times to set it evenly into the mortar.

Variation: For mosaic sheets, use a ³⁄₁₆" V-notched trowel to spread the mortar, and use a grout float to press the sheets into the mortar. Apply pressure gently to avoid creating an uneven surface.

To ensure consistent spacing between tiles, place plastic tile spacers at the corners of the set tile. *Note: With mosaic sheets, use spacers equal to the gaps between tiles.*

5

6

Set tiles into the mortar along the reference lines. Make sure the tiles fit neatly against the spacers. To make sure the tiles are level with one another, lay a straight piece of 2 × 4 across several tiles, and rap the board with a mallet. Lay tile in the remaining area covered with mortar. Repeat steps 1 through 5, working in small sections, until you reach walls or fixtures.

Measure and mark tiles for cutting to fit against walls and into corners, then cut the tiles to fit, following the tips on pages 6 to 11. Apply thinset mortar directly to the back of the cut tiles, instead of the floor, using the notched edge of the trowel to furrow the mortar. Set the tiles.

7

8

9

Measure, cut, and install tiles requiring notches or curves to fit around obstacles, such as exposed pipes or toilet drains.

Remove the spacers with needlenose pliers before the mortar hardens. Inspect the joints and remove high spots of mortar that could show through the grout, using a utility knife. Install tile in the remaining quadrants, completing one quadrant at a time.

Install threshold material in doorways. Set the threshold in thinset mortar so the top is even with the tile. Use the same spacing used for the tiles. Let the mortar cure for at least 24 hours.

(continued)

Mix a small batch of grout, following the manufacturer's directions. (For unglazed or stone tile, add a release agent to prevent the grout from bonding to the tile surfaces.) Starting in a corner, pour the grout over the tile. Spread the grout outward from the corner, pressing firmly on the grout float to completely fill the joints. For best results, tilt the float at a 60° angle to the floor and use a figure-eight motion.

Use the grout float to remove excess grout from the surface of the tile. Wipe diagonally across the joints, holding the float in a nearly vertical position. Continue applying grout and wiping off excess until about 25 sq. ft. of the floor has been grouted.

Remove excess grout by wiping a damp grout sponge diagonally over about 2 sq. ft. of the tile at a time. Rinse the sponge in cool water between wipes. Wipe each area only once; repeated wiping can pull grout from the joints. Repeat steps 10 through 12 to apply grout to the rest of the floor. Allow the grout to dry for about 4 hours, then use a soft cloth to buff the tile surface and remove any remaining grout film.

After the grout has cured completely (check the manufacturer's instructions), apply grout sealer to the grout lines, using a small sponge brush or sash brush. Avoid brushing sealer onto the tile surfaces. Wipe up any excess sealer immediately.

How to Install Base & Trim Tile

1

Dry-fit the trim tiles to determine the best spacing (grout lines in base tile do not always align with grout lines in the floor tile). Use rounded bullnose tiles at outside corners, and mark tiles for cutting as needed.

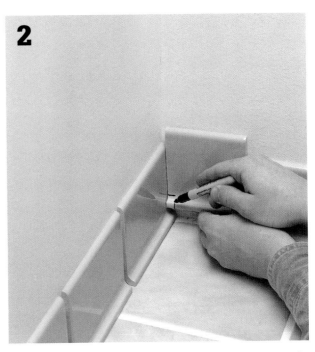

2

Leaving a ⅛" expansion gap between tiles at corners, mark any contour cuts necessary to allow the coved edges to fit together. Use a jigsaw with a tungsten carbide blade to make curved cuts.

3

Begin installing base-trim tiles at an inside corner. Use a notched trowel to apply wall-tile adhesive to the back of each tile. Slip ⅛" spacers under the tiles to create an expansion joint. Set the tiles by pressing them firmly onto the wall.

4

At outside corners, use a double-bullnose tile on one side to cover the edge of the adjoining tile.

5

After the adhesive dries, grout the vertical joints between tiles, and apply grout along the tops of the tiles to make a continuous grout line. After the grout cures, fill the expansion joint at the bottom of the tiles with silicone caulk.

How to Set a Running Bond Tile Pattern

Start running bond tile by dry-fitting tile to establish working reference lines. Dry-fit a few tiles side by side using spacers. Measure the total width of the fitted section (A). Use this measurement to snap a series of equally spaced parallel lines to help keep your tiles straight during installation.

Starting at a point where the layout lines intersect, spread thinset mortar to a small section and lay the first row of tiles. Apply mortar directly to the underside of any tiles that extend outside the mortar bed. Offset the next row by a measurement that's equal to one-half the length of the tile and one-half the width of the grout line.

Continue setting tiles, filling one quadrant at a time. Use the parallel reference lines as guides to keep the rows straight. Immediately wipe away any mortar from the surface of the tiles. When finished, allow the mortar to cure, then grout and clean the tile (see page 44).

How to Set Hexagonal Tile

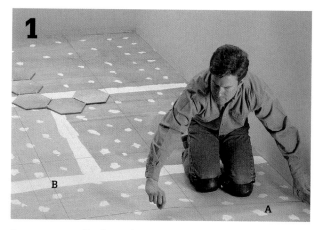

Snap perpendicular reference lines on the underlayment. Lay out three or four tiles in each direction along the layout lines. Place plastic spacers between the tiles to maintain even spacing. Measure the length of this layout in both directions (A and B). Use measurement A to snap a series of equally spaced parallel lines across the entire floor, then do the same for measurement B in the other direction.

Apply thinset mortar to small sections at a time and begin setting tile. Apply mortar directly to the underside of any tiles that extend outside the mortar bed. Continue setting the tiles, using the grid layout and spacers to keep the tiles aligned. Wipe off any mortar from the tile surface. When finished, allow the mortar to set, then grout.

How to Set a Diagonal Pattern within a Border

Plan your border layout in the room (see pages 28 to 34). Dry-fit border tiles with spacers in the planned area. Make sure the border tiles are aligned with the reference lines. Dry-fit tiles at the outside corners of the border arrangement. Adjust the tile positions as necessary to create a layout with minimal cutting. When the layout of the tiles is set, snap chalk lines around the border tiles and trace along the edges of the outside tiles. Install the border tiles.

Draw diagonal layout lines at a 45° angle to the perpendicular reference lines.

Use standard tile-setting techniques to set field tiles inside the border. Kneel on a wide board to distribute your weight if you need to work in a tiled area that has not cured overnight.

15. Installing a Glass Mosaic Floor

Throughout history, mosaic tile has been more than a floor or wall covering—it's been an art form. In fact, the Latin origins of the word mosaic refer to art "worthy of the muses." Mosaic tile is beautiful and durable, and working with it is easier than ever today. Modern mosaic floor tile is available in squares that are held together by an underlayer of fabric mesh. These squares are set in much the same way as larger tile, but their flexibility makes them slightly more difficult to hold, place, and move. The instructions given with this project simplify the handling of these squares.

Some manufacturers stabilize mosaic squares with a paper facing on the front of the square. Most facings of this type can be removed with warm water, which we describe here. However, this can vary, so be sure to read and follow manufacturer's recommendations regarding this facing and its removal.

The colors of mosaic tile shift just as much as any other tile, so make sure all the boxes you buy are from the same lot and batch. Colors often vary from one box to another, too, but mixing tile from boxes makes any shifts less noticeable.

It's also important to know that adhesive made for other tile may not work with glass or specialty mosaic tile. Consult your tile retailer for advice on the right mortar or mastic for your project. Before you start, clean and prepare the floor. Measure the room and draw reference lines (page 31). Lay out sheets of tile along both the vertical and horizontal reference lines. If these lines will produce small or difficult cuts at the edges, shift them until you're satisfied with the layout.

Tools & Materials ▸

Tape measure	Mosaic tile
Chalk line	Tile adhesive
¼" notched trowel	Tile spacers
Grout float	Grout
Grout sponge	Latex additive
Buff rag	Grout sealer
Sponge applicator	Tile clippers
Needlenose pliers	2 × 4

How to Install a Glass Mosaic Floor

Beginning at the intersection of the horizontal and vertical lines, apply the recommended adhesive in one quadrant. Spread it outward evenly with a notched trowel. Lay down only as much adhesive as you can cover in 10 to 15 minutes.

Stabilize a sheet of tile by randomly inserting three or four plastic spacers into the open joints.

Pick up diagonally opposite corners of the square and move it to the intersection of the horizontal and vertical references lines. Align the sides with the reference lines and gently press one corner into place on the adhesive. Slowly lower the opposite corner, making sure the sides remain square with the reference lines. Massage the sheet into the adhesive, being careful not to press too hard or twist the sheet out of position. Continue setting tile, filling in one square area after another.

(continued)

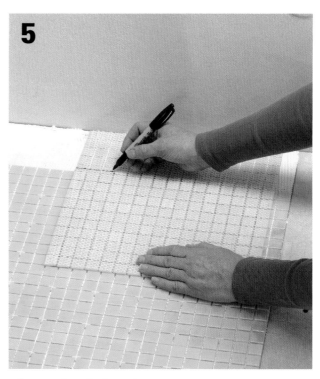

When two or three sheets are in place, lay a scrap of 2 × 4 wrapped in carpet across them and tap it with a rubber mallet to set the fabric mesh into the adhesive and force out any trapped air.

When you've tiled up close to the wall or another boundary, lay a full mosaic sheet into position and mark it for trimming. If you've planned well and are installing small-tile mosaics, you can often avoid the need to cut tiles.

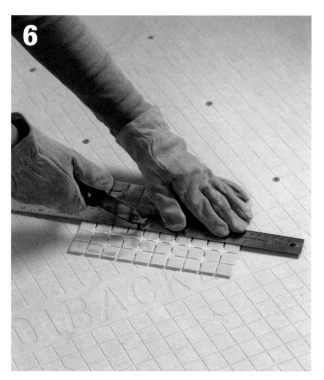

If you do need to cut tiles in the mosaic sheet, and not just the backing, score the tiles with a tile cutter. Be sure the tiles are still attached to the backing. Add spacers between the individual tiles to prevent them from shifting as you score.

After you've scored the tiles, cut them each individually with a pair of tile nippers.

8

Set tile in the remaining quadrants. Let the adhesive cure according to the manufacturer's instructions. Remove spacers with a needlenose pliers. Mix a batch of grout and fill the joints (see page 44). Allow the grout to dry, according to manufacturer's instructions.

9

Mosaic tile has a much higher ratio of grout to tile than larger tiles do, so it is especially important to seal the grout with a quality sealer after it has cured.

Working Around Obstacles ▸

1

To work around pipes and other obstructions, cut through the backing to create an access point for the sheet. Then, remove the tiles within the mosaic sheet to clear a space large enough for the pipe or other obstruction.

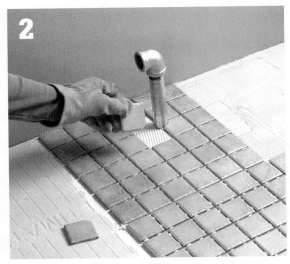

2

Set the cut sheet into an adhesive bed, and then cut small pieces of tile and fit them into the layout as necessary.

16. Building a Tiled Shower Base

Building a custom-tiled shower base lets you choose the shape and size of your shower rather than having its dimensions dictated by available products. Building the base is quite simple, though it does require time and some knowledge of basic masonry techniques because the base is formed primarily using mortar. What you get for your time and trouble can be spectacular.

Before designing a shower base, contact your local building department regarding code restrictions and to secure the necessary permits. Most codes require water controls to be accessible from outside the shower and describe acceptable door positions and operation. Requirements like these influence the size and position of the base.

Choosing the tile before finalizing the design lets you size the base to require mostly full tile. Showers are among the most frequently used amenities in the average home, so it really makes sense to build one that is comfortable and pleasing to your senses. Consider using small tile and gradate the color from top to bottom or in a sweep across the walls. Or, use trim tile and listellos on the walls to create an interesting focal point.

Whatever tile you choose, remember to seal the grout in your new shower and to maintain it carefully over the years. Full, water-resistant grout protects the structure of the shower and prolongs its useful life.

Tools & Materials ▸

Tape measure
Circular saw
Hammer
Utility knife
Stapler
2-ft. level
Mortar mixing box
Trowel
Wood float
Felt-tip marker
Ratchet wrench
Expandable stopper
Drill
Tin snips
Torpedo level
Tools for installing tile (page 56)
2 × 4 and 2 × 10 framing lumber
16d galvanized common nails
15# building paper
Staples

3-piece shower drain
PVC primer
PVC cement
Galvanized finish nails
Galvanized metal lath
Thick-bed floor mortar ("deck mud")
Latex mortar additive
Laminating adhesive
CPE waterproof membrane & preformed dam corners
CPE membrane solvent glue
CPE membrane sealant
Cementboard and materials for installing cementboard
Materials for installing tile

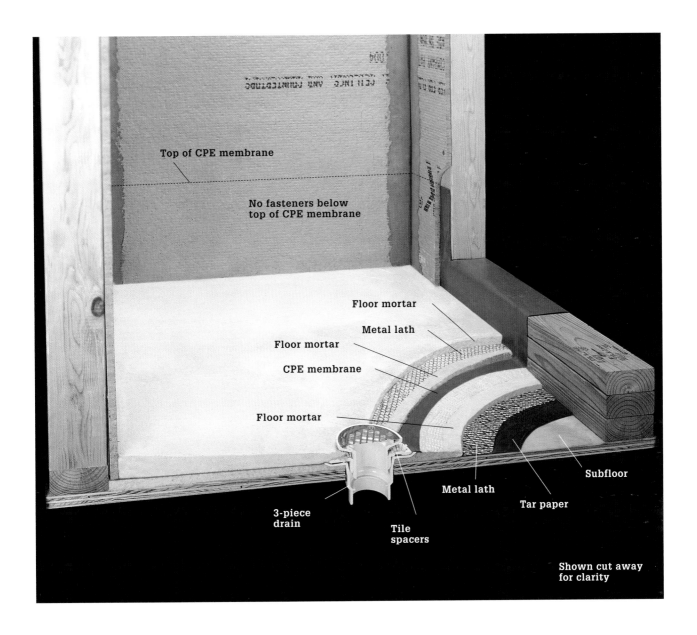

Top of CPE membrane

No fasteners below
top of CPE membrane

Floor mortar

Metal lath

Floor mortar

CPE membrane

Floor mortar

Subfloor

Metal lath

Tar paper

3-piece
drain

Tile
spacers

Shown cut away
for clarity

Tips for Building a Custom Shower Base ▸

A custom-tiled shower base is built in three layers to ensure proper water drainage: the pre pan, the shower pan, and the shower floor. A mortar pre pan is first built on top of the subfloor, establishing a slope toward the drain of ¼" for every 12" of shower floor. Next, a waterproof chlorinated polyethylene (CPE) membrane forms the shower pan, providing a watertight seal for the shower base. Finally, a second mortar bed reinforced with wire mesh is installed for the shower floor, providing a surface for tile installation. If water penetrates the tiled shower floor, the shower pan and sloped pre pan will direct it to the weep holes of the 3-piece drain.

    One of the most important steps in building a custom-tiled shower base is testing the shower pan after installation (step 13). This allows you to locate and fix any leaks to prevent costly damage.

How to Build a Custom-tiled Shower Base

Remove building materials to expose subfloor and stud walls. Cut three 2 × 4s for the curb and fasten them to the floor joists and the studs at the shower threshold with 16d galvanized common nails. Also cut 2 × 10 lumber to size and install in the stud bays around the perimeter of the shower base.

Staple 15# building paper to the subfloor of the shower base. Disassemble the 3-piece shower drain and glue the bottom piece to the drain pipe with PVC cement. Partially screw the drain bolts into the drain piece, and stuff a rag into the drain pipe to prevent mortar from falling into the drain.

Mark the height of the bottom drain piece on the wall farthest from the center of the drain. Measure from the center of the drain straight across to that wall, then raise the height mark ¼" for every 12" of shower floor to slope the pre pan toward the drain. Trace a reference line at the height mark around the perimeter of the entire alcove, using a level.

Staple galvanized metal lath over the building paper; cut a hole in the lath ½" from the drain. Mix floor mortar (or "deck mud") to a fairly dry consistency, using a latex additive for strength; mortar should hold its shape when squeezed (inset). Trowel the mortar onto the subfloor, building the pre pan from the flange of the drain piece to the height line on the perimeter of the walls.

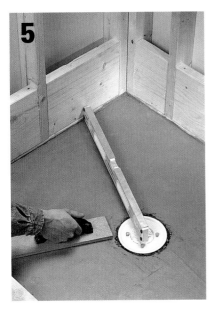

Continue using the trowel to form the pre pan, checking the slope using a level and filling any low spots with mortar. Finish the surface of the pre pan with a wood float until it is even and smooth. Allow the mortar to cure overnight.

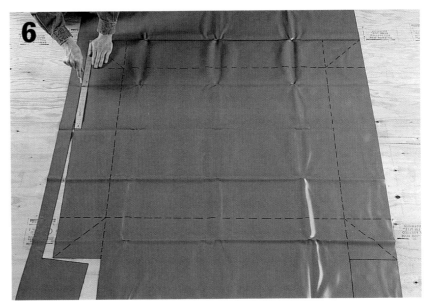

Measure the dimensions of the shower floor, and mark it out on a sheet of CPE waterproof membrane, using a felt-tipped marker. From the floor outline, measure out and mark an additional 8" for each wall and 16" for the curb end. Cut the membrane to size, using a utility knife and straightedge. Be careful to cut on a clean, smooth surface to prevent puncturing the membrane. Lay the membrane onto the shower pan.

Measure to find the exact location of the drain and mark it on the membrane, outlining the outer diameter of the drain flange. Cut a circular piece of CPE membrane roughly 2" larger than the drain flange, then use CPE membrane solvent glue to weld it into place and reinforce the seal at the drain.

Apply CPE sealant around the drain. Fold the membrane along the floor outline. Set the membrane over the pre pan so the reinforced drain seal is centered over the drain bolts. Working from the drain to the walls, carefully tuck the membrane tight into each corner, folding the extra material into triangular flaps.

(continued)

9

Apply CPE solvent glue to one side, press the flap flat, then staple it in place. Staple only the top edge of the membrane to the blocking; do not staple below the top of the curb, or on the curb itself.

10

At the shower curb, cut the membrane along the studs so it can be folded over the curb. Solvent-glue a dam corner at each inside corner of the curb. Do not fasten the dam corners with staples.

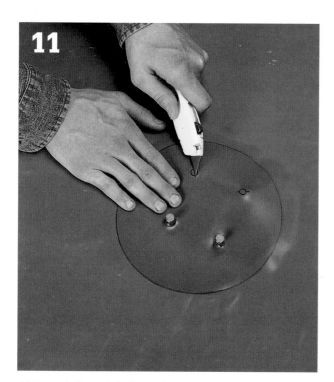

11

At the reinforced drain seal on the membrane, locate and mark the drain bolts. Press the membrane down around the bolts, then use a utility knife to carefully cut a slit just large enough for the bolts to poke through. Push the membrane down over the bolts.

12

Use a utility knife to carefully cut away only enough of the membrane to expose the drain and allow the middle drain piece to fit in place. Remove the drain bolts, then position the middle drain piece over the bolt holes. Reinstall the bolts, tightening them evenly and firmly to create a watertight seal.

Test the shower pan for leaks overnight. Place a balloon tester in the drain below the weep holes, and fill the pan with water, to 1" below the top of the curb. Mark the water level and let the water sit overnight. If the water level remains the same, the pan holds water. If the level is lower, locate and fix leaks in the pan using patches of membrane and CPE solvent.

Install cementboard on the alcove walls, using ¼" wood shims to lift the bottom edge off the CPE membrane. To prevent puncturing the membrane, do not use fasteners in the lower 8" of the cementboard. Cut a piece of metal lath to fit around the three sides of the curb. Bend the lath so it tightly conforms to the curb. Pressing the lath against the top of the curb, staple it to the outside face of the curb. Mix enough mortar for the two sides of the curb.

Overhang the front edge of the curb with a straight 1× board, so it is flush with the outer wall material. Apply mortar to the mesh with a trowel, building to the edge of the board. Clear away excess mortar, then use a torpedo level to check for plumb, making adjustments as needed. Repeat for the inside face of the curb. *Note: The top of the curb will be finished after tile is installed (step 19). Allow the mortar to cure overnight.*

Attach the drain strainer piece to the drain, adjusting it to a minimum of 1½" above the shower pan. On one wall, mark 1½" up from the shower pan, then use a level to draw a reference line around the perimeter of the shower base. Because the pre pan establishes the ¼" per foot slope, this measurement will maintain that slope.

(continued)

17

Spread tile spacers over the weep holes of the drain to prevent mortar from plugging the holes. Mix the floor mortar, then build up the shower floor to roughly half the thickness of the base. Cut metal lath to cover the mortar bed, keeping it ½" from the drain (see photo in step 18).

18

Continue to add mortar, building the floor to the reference line on the walls. Use a level to check the slope, and pack mortar into low spots with a trowel. Leave space at the drain for the thickness of the tile. Float the surface using a wood float until it is smooth and slopes evenly to the drain. When finished, allow the mortar to cure overnight before installing the tiles.

19

After the floor has cured, draw reference lines and establish the tile layout, then mix a batch of thinset mortar and install the floor tile (pages 40 to 47). At the curb, cut the tiles for the inside to protrude ½" above the unfinished top of the curb, and the tiles for the outside to protrude ⅝" above the top, establishing a ⅛" slope so water drains back into the shower. Use a level to check the tops of the tiles for level as you work.

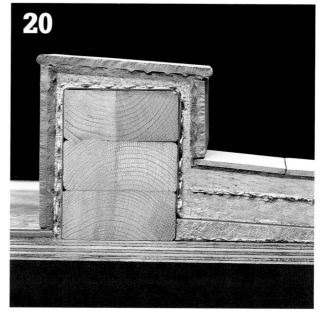

20

Mix enough floor mortar to cover the unfinished top of the curb, then pack it in place between the tiles, using a trowel. Screed off the excess mortar flush with the tops of the side tiles. Allow the mortar to cure, then install bullnose cap tile. Install the wall tile, then grout, clean, and seal all the tile (page 44). After the grout has cured fully, run a bead of silicone caulk around all inside corners to create control joints.

Textured surfaces improve the safety of tile floors, especially in wet areas such as this open shower. The shower area is designated effectively by a simple shift in color and size.

The raised curb on this open shower keeps most of the water headed toward the drain. But no matter, the entire bathroom is tiled, so stray droplets are no problem.

Mosaic tile, with its mesh backing and small shapes, often works well on curved walls such as the one that forms this shower. The rectangular shape of the individual mosaic tiles complements the shape of the post at the corner of the shower.

17. Installing a Tile Wall

Tile is an ideal covering for walls in kitchens and bathrooms, but there's no reason to limit its use to those rooms. It's not as common in North American homes, but in Europe tile has been used in rooms throughout the house for generations. And why not? Beautiful, practical, easy to clean and maintain, tile walls are well suited to many spaces. On the preceding pages, you've seen some design ideas for tile walls. Now it's time to get down to business.

When shopping for tile, keep in mind that tiles that are at least 6" × 6" are easier to install than small tiles, because they require less cutting and cover more surface area. Larger tiles also have fewer grout lines that must be cleaned and maintained. Check out the selection of trim and specialty tiles and ceramic accessories that are available to help you customize your project.

Most wall tile is designed to have narrow grout lines (less than ⅛" wide) filled with unsanded grout. Grout lines wider than ⅛" should be filled with sanded floor-tile grout. Either type will last longer if it contains, or is mixed with, a latex additive. To prevent staining, it's a good idea to seal your grout after it fully cures, then once a year thereafter.

You can use standard drywall or water-resistant drywall (called "greenboard") as a backer for walls in dry areas. In wet areas, install tile over cementboard. Made from cement and fiberglass, cementboard cannot be damaged by water, though moisture can pass through it. To protect the framing, install a waterproof membrane, such as roofing felt or polyethylene sheeting, between the framing members and the cementboard. Be sure to tape and finish the seams between cementboard panels before laying the tile.

See page 35 for information on planning and laying out tile walls.

Tools & Materials ▸

Tile-cutting tools	Dry-set tile mortar
Marker	with latex additive
Tape measure	Ceramic wall tile
4-ft. level	Ceramic trim tile
Notched trowel	(as needed)
Mallet	2 × 4
Grout float	Carpet scrap
Grout sponge	Tile grout with latex
Soft cloth	additive
Small paintbrush	Tub & tile caulk
or foam brush	Alkaline grout sealer
Caulk gun	Cardboard
Straight 1 × 2	Story stick/pole

How to Set Wall Tile

Design the layout and mark the reference lines (see pages 29 to 32). Begin installation with the second row of tiles above the floor. If the layout requires cut tiles for this row, mark and cut the tiles for the entire row at one time.

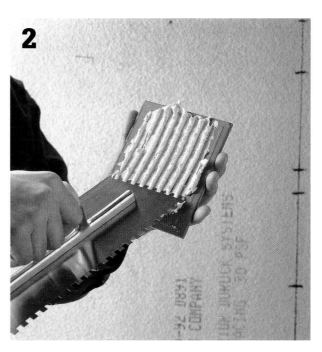

Mix a small batch of thinset mortar containing a latex additive. (Some mortar has additive mixed in by the manufacturer and some must have additive mixed in separately.) Cover the back of the first tile with adhesive, using a ¼" notched trowel.

Variation: Spread adhesive on a small section of the wall, then set the tiles into the adhesive. Thinset adhesive sets quickly, so work quickly if you choose this installation method.

Beginning near the center of the wall, apply the tile to the wall with a slight twisting motion, aligning it exactly with the horizontal and vertical reference lines. When placing cut tiles, position the cut edges where they will be least visible.

(continued)

Continue installing tiles, working from the center to the sides in a pyramid pattern. Keep the tiles aligned with the reference lines. If the tiles are not self-spacing, use plastic spacers inserted in the corner joints to maintain even grout lines. The base row should be the last row of full tiles installed. Cut tile as necessary (see pages 6 to 11).

As small sections of tile are completed, "set" the tile by laying a scrap of 2 × 4 wrapped with carpet onto the tile and rapping it lightly with a mallet. This embeds the tile solidly in the adhesive and creates a flat, even surface.

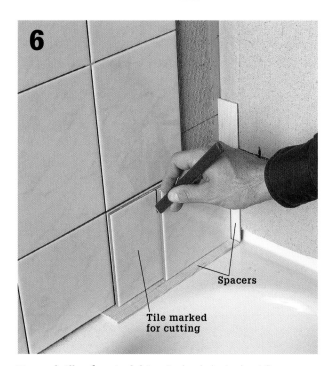

Spacers

Tile marked for cutting

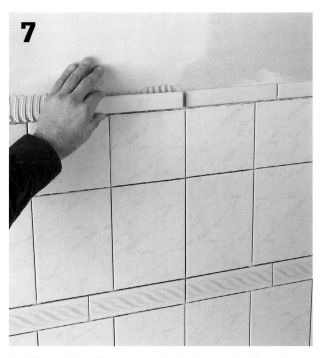

To mark tiles for straight cuts, begin by taping ⅛" spacers against the surfaces below and to the side of the tile. Position a tile directly over the last full tile installed, then place a third tile so the edge butts against the spacers. Trace the edge of the top tile onto the middle tile to mark it for cutting.

Install any trim tiles, such as the bullnose edge tiles shown above, at border areas. Wipe away excess mortar along the top edges of the edge tiles. Use bullnose and corner bullnose (with two adjacent bullnose edges) tiles at outside corners to cover the rough edges of the adjoining tiles.

8

Let mortar dry completely (12 to 24 hours), then mix a batch of grout containing latex additive. Apply the grout with a rubber grout float, using a sweeping motion to force it deep into the joints. Do not grout joints adjoining bathtubs, floors, or room corners. These will serve as expansion joints and will be caulked later.

9

Wipe a damp grout sponge diagonally over the tile, rinsing the sponge in cool water between wipes. Wipe each area only once; repeated wiping can pull grout from the joints. Allow the grout to dry for about 4 hours, then use a soft cloth to buff the tile surface and remove any remaining grout film.

10

When the grout has cured completely, use a small foam brush to apply grout sealer to the joints, following the manufacturer's directions. Avoid brushing sealer on the tile surfaces, and wipe up excess sealer immediately.

11

Seal expansion joints at the floor and corners with silicone caulk. After the caulk dries, buff the tile with a dry, soft cloth.

How to Install Wall Tile in a Bathtub Alcove

Beginning with the back wall, measure up and mark a point at a distance equal to the height of one ceramic tile (if the tub edge is not level, measure up from the lowest spot). Draw a level line through this point, along the entire back wall. This line represents a tile grout line and will be used as a reference line for making the entire tile layout.

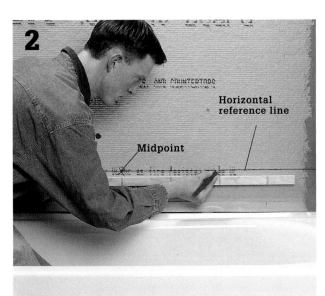

Measure and mark the midpoint on the horizontal reference line. Using a story stick, mark along the reference line where the vertical grout joints will be located. If the story stick shows that the corner tiles will be less than half of a full tile width, move the midpoint half the width of a tile in either direction and mark (shown in next step).

Use a level to draw a vertical reference line through the adjusted midpoint from the tub edge to the ceiling. Measure up from the tub edge along the vertical reference line and mark the rough height of the top row of tiles.

Use the story stick to mark the horizontal grout joints along the vertical reference line, beginning at the mark for the top row of tiles. If the cut tiles at the tub edge will be less than half the height of a full tile, move the top row up half the height of a tile. *Note: If tiling to a ceiling, evenly divide the tiles to be cut at the ceiling and tub edge, as for the corner tiles.*

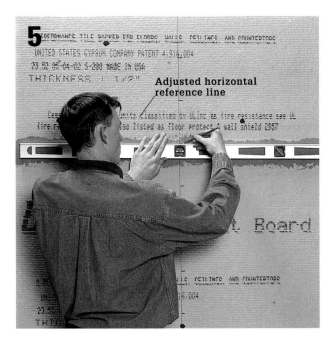

Use a level to draw an adjusted horizontal reference line through the vertical reference line at a grout joint mark close to the center of the layout. This splits the tile area into four workable quadrants.

Use a level to transfer the adjusted horizontal reference line from the back wall to both side walls, then follow step 3 through step 6 to lay out both side walls. Adjust the layout as needed so the final column of tiles ends at the outside edge of the tub. Use only the adjusted horizontal and vertical reference lines for ceramic tile installation.

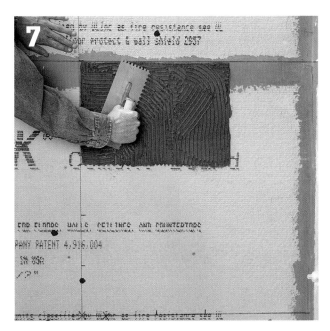

Mix a small batch of thinset mortar containing a latex additive. (Some mortar has additive mixed in by the manufacturer and some must have additive mixed separately.) Spread adhesive on a small section of the wall, along both legs of one quadrant, using a ¼" notched trowel.

Use the edge of the trowel to create furrows in the mortar. Set the first tile in the corner of the quadrant where the lines intersect, using a slight twisting motion. Align the tile exactly with both reference lines. When placing cut tiles, position the cut edges where they will be least visible.

Continue installing tiles, working from the center out into the field of the quadrant. Keep the tiles aligned with the reference lines and tile in one quadrant at a time. If the tiles are not self-spacing, use plastic spacers inserted in the corner joints to maintain even grout lines (inset). The base row against the tub edge should be the last row of tiles installed.

Install trim tiles, such as the bullnose tiles shown above, at border areas. Wipe away excess mortar along the top edges of the edge tiles.

Mark and cut tiles to fit around all plumbing accessories or plumbing fixtures. Refer to pages 6 to 11 for tile cutting techniques.

Install any ceramic accessories by applying thinset mortar to the back side, then pressing the accessory into place. Use masking tape to support the weight until the mortar dries (inset). Fill the tub with water, then seal expansion joints around the bathtub, floor, and corners with silicone caulk.

Variation: Tiling Bathroom Walls

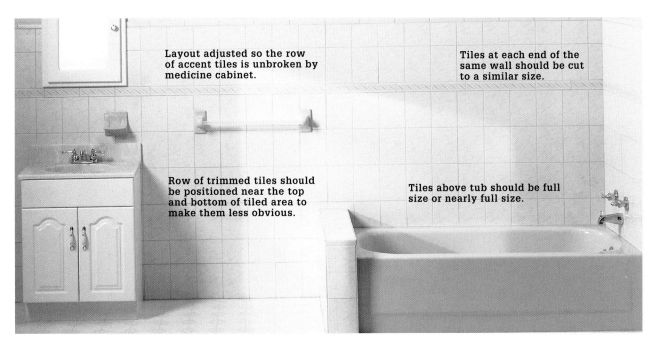

Layout adjusted so the row of accent tiles is unbroken by medicine cabinet.

Tiles at each end of the same wall should be cut to a similar size.

Row of trimmed tiles should be positioned near the top and bottom of tiled area to make them less obvious.

Tiles above tub should be full size or nearly full size.

Tiling an entire bathroom requires careful planning. The bathroom shown here was designed so that the tiles directly above the bathtub (the most visible surface) are nearly full height. To accomplish this, cut tiles were used in the second row up from the floor. The short second row also allows the row of accent tiles to run uninterrupted below the medicine cabinet. Cut tiles in both corners should be of similar width to maintain a symmetrical look in the room.

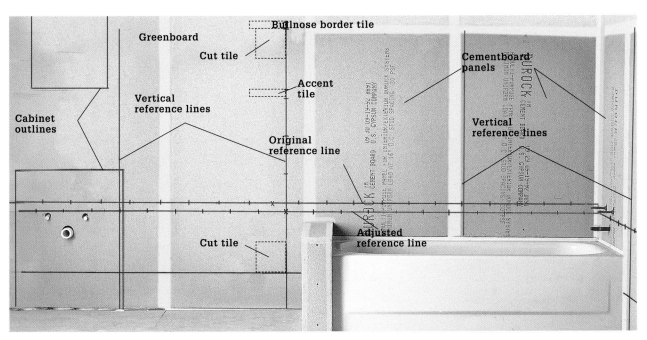

Greenboard

Bullnose border tile

Cut tile

Cementboard panels

Cabinet outlines

Vertical reference lines

Accent tile

Original reference line

Vertical reference lines

Cut tile

Adjusted reference line

The key to a successful wall-tile project is the layout. Mark the wall to show the planned location of all wall cabinets, fixtures, and wall accessories, then locate the most visible horizontal line in the bathroom, which is usually the top edge of the bathtub. Follow the steps on pages 28 to 34 to establish the layout, using a story stick to see how the tile pattern will run in relation to the other features in the room. After establishing the working reference lines, mark additional vertical reference lines on the walls every 5 to 6 tile spaces along the adjusted horizontal reference line to split large walls into smaller, workable quadrants, then install the tile. *Note: Premixed, latex mastic adhesives generally are acceptable for wall tile in dry areas.*

18. Tiling a Kitchen Backsplash

There are few spaces in your home with as much potential for creativity and visual impact as the 18" between your kitchen countertop and cupboards. A well-designed backsplash can transform an ordinary kitchen into something extraordinary. Tiles for the backsplash can be attached directly to wallboard or plaster and do not require backerboard. When purchasing the tile, order 10 percent extra to cover breakage and cutting. Before installing, prepare the work area by removing switch and receptacle coverplates. Protect the countertop from scratches by covering it with a drop cloth.

Tools & Materials ▸

Level	Straight 1 × 2
Tape measure	Wall tile
Pencil	Tile spacers
Tile cutter	(if needed)
Rod saw	Bullnose trim tile
Notched trowel	Mastic tile adhesive
Rubber grout float	Masking tape
Beating block	Grout
Rubber mallet	Caulk
Sponge	Drop cloth
Bucket	Grout sealer

Tips for Planning Tile Layouts ▸

Gather planning brochures and design catalogs to help you create decorative patterns and borders for the backsplash.

Break tiles into fragments and make a mosaic backsplash. Always use a sanded grout for joints wider than ⅛".

Add painted mural tiles to create a focal point. Mixing various tile styles adds an appealing contrast.

How to Tile a Backsplash

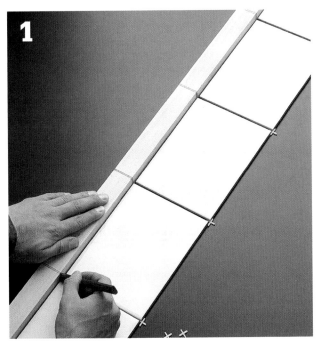

Make a story stick by marking a board at least half as long as the backsplash area to match the tile spacing.

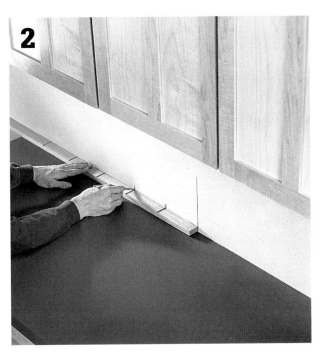

Starting at the midpoint of the installation area, use the story stick to make layout marks along the wall. If an end piece is too small (less than half a tile), adjust the midpoint to give you larger, more attractive end pieces. Use a level to mark this point with a vertical reference line.

While it may appear straight, your countertop may not be level and therefore is not a reliable reference line. Run a level along the counter to find the lowest point on the countertop. Mark a point two tiles up from the low point and extend a level line across the entire work area.

(continued)

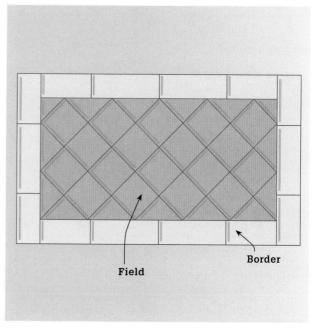

Variation: Diagonal layout. Mark vertical and horizontal reference lines, making sure the angle is 90°. To establish diagonal layout lines, measure out equal distances from the crosspoint, then connect the points with a line. Additional layout lines can be extended from these as needed. To avoid the numerous, unattractive perimeter cuts common to diagonal layouts, try using a standard border pattern as shown. Diagonally set a field of full tiles only, then cut enough half tiles to fill out the perimeter. Finally, border the diagonal field with tiles set square to the field.

4

Apply mastic adhesive evenly to the area beneath the horizontal reference line, using a notched trowel. Comb the adhesive horizontally with the notched edge.

5

Starting at the vertical reference line, press tiles into the adhesive with a slight twisting motion. If the tiles are not self-spacing, use plastic spacers to maintain even grout lines. If the tiles do not hang in place, use masking tape to hold them in place until the adhesive sets.

6

Install a whole row along the reference line, checking occasionally to make sure the tiles are level. Continue installing tiles below the first row, trimming tiles that butt against the countertop as needed.

7

Apply adhesive to an area above the line and continue placing tiles, working from the center to the sides. Install trim tile, such as bullnose tile, to the edges of the rows.

8

When the tiles are in place, make sure they are flat and firmly embedded by laying a beating block against the tile and rapping it lightly with a mallet. Remove the spacers. Allow the mastic to dry for at least 24 hours, or as directed by the manufacturer.

9

Mix the grout and apply it with a rubber grout float. Spread it over the tiles, keeping the float at a low 30° angle, pressing the grout deep into the joints. *Note: For grout joints ⅛" and smaller, be sure to use a non-sanded grout.*

10

Wipe off excess grout, holding the float at a right angle to the tile, working diagonally so as not to remove grout from the joints. Clean any remaining grout from the tiles with a damp sponge, working in a circular motion. Rinse the sponge thoroughly and often.

11

Shape the grout joints by making slow, short, passes with the sponge, shaving down any high spots; rinse the sponge frequently. Fill any voids by applying a dab of grout with your fingertip. When the grout has dried to a haze, buff the tile clean with a soft cloth. Apply a bead of caulk between the countertop and tiles. Reinstall any electrical fixtures you removed. After the grout has completely cured, you may want to apply a grout sealer to help prevent discoloration.

19. Building a Tiled Tub Deck

The aprons that are cast into alcove bathtubs simplify the tub installation, but they often come up a bit short in the style department. One way to improve the appearance of a plain apron and create the look of a built-in tub is simply to build and tile a short wall in front of the tub. All it takes is a little simple framing and a few square feet of tile.

The basic strategy is to construct a 2 × 4 stub wall in front of the tub apron and then tile the top and front of the wall. One design option is to try and match existing tile, but it's unlikely you'll be able to find the exact tile unless it's relatively new. Choosing complementary or contrasting tile is usually a better bet. Specialty tile, such as listellos, pencils, and accent tile, can create a lot of impact without breaking the bank because you're covering such a small area. Ask your tile retailer to direct you to families of tile with multiple shapes and accessories.

Be sure to include a waterproof backer (cementboard is recommended) and get a good grout seal, since the stub wall will be in a wet area.

Tools & Materials ▸

Stud finder
Tape measure
Circular saw
Drill
Hammer
Laser or
    carpenter's level
Tile cutting tools
Utility knife
Grout float
Grout sponge
Buff rag
Foam brush
2 × 4 lumber
Construction adhesive
2½" screws

Cementboard
Drywall screws
Tile
Thinset mortar
Scrap of carpet
Carbide paper
    or wet stone
Wide painter's tape
Grout
Silicone caulk
Grout sealer
Permanent marker
Notched trowel
Rubbing alcohol

How to Build a Tiled Tub Deck

Measure the distance of the tub rim from the floor, as well as the distance from one wall to the other at the ends of the tub. Allowing for the thickness of the tiles, create a layout for the project and draw a detailed plan for your project, spacing the studs 16" apart on center.

Cut the 2 × 4s to length for the base plate and top plate (58½" long as shown). Cut the studs (five 11" pieces as shown). Set the base plate on edge and lay out the studs, spacing them 16" on center. Make sure the first and last studs are perfectly parallel with the end of the base plate, then drive two 2½" screws through the base plate and each stud.

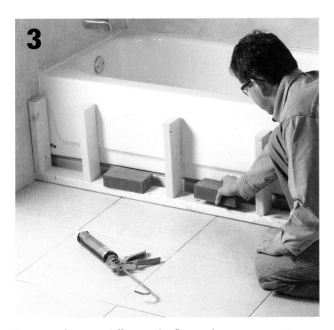

Draw a placement line on the floor, using a permanent marker. Spread a generous bead of construction adhesive on the bottom of the base plate. Align the base plate with the placement line and set it into position. Put concrete blocks or other weights between the studs to anchor the base plate to the flooring and let the adhesive cure according to manufacturer's instructions.

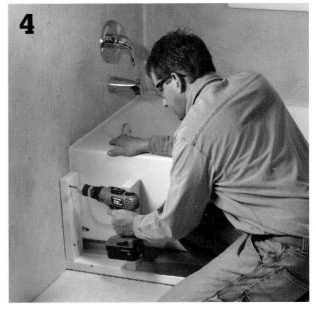

Drive two or three 2½" screws through the studs and into the room walls at each end of the stub wall. If the stub wall does not happen to line up with any wall studs, at least drive two 3" deck screws toenail style through the stub wall and into the room wall sole plate.

(continued)

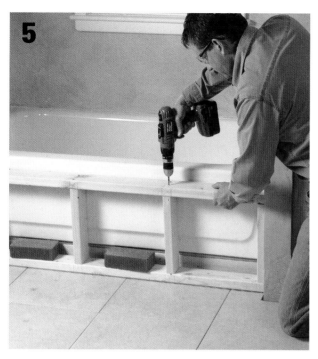

Set the top plate on the stud wall and attach it, using two 2½" screws for each stud. Offset the screws slightly to increase the strength of the assembly. The top of the stud wall should be 2½" below the top of the tub.

Cut cementboard to fit the front (14½" as shown). With the factory-finished edge of the cementboard at the top of the wall, attach the cementboard to the studs, using drywall screws (see page 24).

Cut cementboard to fit the top of the stub wall (3½"). With the factory-finished edge facing the tub edge, attach the cement board to the top plate, using drywall screws.

Design the layout and mark reference lines (see page 31) on the wall. Draw horizontal and vertical reference lines for the corner tile (used to transition from vertical to horizontal at the top stub wall edge) and the coved base tile (if your project includes them, as ours does). Lay out tile along the floor, including spacers.

Start tiling at the bottom of the wall. Lay out the bottom row of tile on the floor, using spacers if necessary. Adjust the layout to make end tiles balanced in size. Mark and cut the tiles as necessary, and then smooth any sharp edges with carbide paper or a wet stone. Mix a small batch of thinset mortar (see page 12) and install the base tiles by buttering the backs with mortar (see page 13).

Beginning at the center intersection of the vertical field area, apply mortar, using a notched trowel to spread it evenly. Cover as much area as required for a few field tiles. Install the field tiles, keeping the grout lines in alignment.

Finish installing the field tiles up to the horizontal line marking the accent tile location.

Apply thinset mortar to the backs of the accent tiles and install them in a straight line. The grout lines will likely not align with the field tile grout lines.

(continued)

Install corner tiles to create a rounded transition at the top edge of the wall. Install these before you install the filed tiles in the top row of the wall face or on the top of the stub wall (corner tiles are virtually impossible to cut if your measurements are off). Dry-lay the top row of tiles. Mark and cut tile if necessary.

Fill in the top course of field tile on the wall face, between the accent tiles and the corner tiles. If you have planned well you won't need to trim the field tiles to fit. (If you need to cut tiles to create the correct wall height, choose the tiles in the first row of field tiles.)

Remove the dry-lay row of tile along the top of the wall. Shield the edge of the tub with painter's tape, then spread thinset adhesive on the wall and begin to lay tile. Keep the joints of the field tiles on the top aligned with the grout joints of the field tile on the face of the wall.

Mix a batch of grout and use a grout float to force it into the joints between the tiles. Keep the space between the top field tiles and the tub clear of grout to create space for a bead of silicone caulk between the tub and tile.

Remove excess grout and clean the tile using a damp sponge. Rinse the sponge often.

After 24 hours, clean the area where the tile and tub meet with rubbing alcohol, then put tape on the edge of the tub and the face of the tile. Apply clear silicone caulk into the gap, overfilling it slightly.

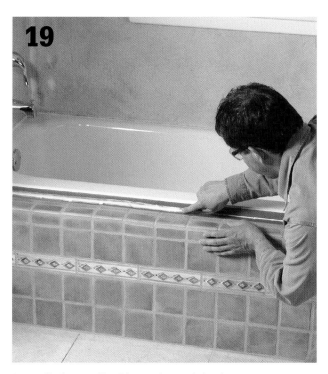

Smooth the caulk with a moistened plastic straw or a moistened fingertip to create an even finish. Make sure this spot is well-sealed, as it is a prime spot for water to penetrate into the tub wall.

When the grout has cured completely (consult manufacturer's directions), apply grout sealer to the joints.

20. Building a Tile Countertop

Ceramic and porcelain tile remain popular choices for countertops and backsplashes for a number of reasons: It's available in a vast range of sizes, styles, and colors; it's durable and repairable; and some tile—not all—is reasonably priced. With careful planning, tile is also easy to install, making a custom countertop a good do-it-yourself project.

The best tile for most countertops is glazed ceramic or porcelain floor tile. Glazed tile is better than unglazed because of its stain resistance, and floor tile is better than wall tile because it's thicker and more durable.

While glazing protects tile from stains, the grout between tiles is still vulnerable because it's so porous. To minimize staining, use a grout that contains a latex additive, or mix the grout using a liquid latex additive. After the grout cures fully, apply a quality grout sealer, and reapply the sealer once a year thereafter. Choosing larger tiles reduces the number of grout lines. Although the selection is a bit limited, if you choose 13" × 13" floor tile, you can span from the front to the back edge of the countertop with a single seam.

The countertop in this project has a substrate of ¾" exterior-grade plywood that's cut to fit and fastened to the cabinets. The plywood is covered with a layer of plastic (for a moisture barrier) and a layer of ½"-thick cementboard. Cementboard is an effective backer for tile because it won't break down if water gets through the tile layer. The tile is adhered to the cementboard with thinset adhesive. The overall thickness of the finished countertop is about 1½". If you want a thicker countertop, you can fasten an additional layer of plywood (of any thickness) beneath the substrate. Two layers of ¾" exterior-grade plywood without cementboard is also an acceptable substrate.

You can purchase tiles made specifically to serve as backsplashes and front edging. While the color and texture may match, these tiles usually come in only one length, making it difficult to get your grout lines to align with the field tiles. You can solve this problem by cutting your own edging and backsplash tiles from field tiles (see step 5, page 70).

Tools & Materials ▶

Tape measure	Tile spacers
Circular saw	¾" exterior-grade
Drill	(CDX) plywood
Utility knife	4-mil polyethylene
Straightedge	sheeting
Stapler	Packing tape
Drywall knife	½" cementboard
Framing square	1¼" galvanized deck screws
Notched trowel	Fiberglass mesh tape
Tile cutter	Thinset mortar
Carpeted 2 × 4	Grout with latex additive
Mallet	Silicone caulk
Rubber grout float	Silicone grout sealer
Sponge	Tile saw
Foam brush	Grout float
Caulk gun	Metal ruler
Ceramic tile	Writing utensil

Ceramic or porcelain makes a durable countertop that is heat-resistant and relatively easy for a DIYer to create. By using larger tiles, you minimize the grout lines (and the cleaning that goes with them).

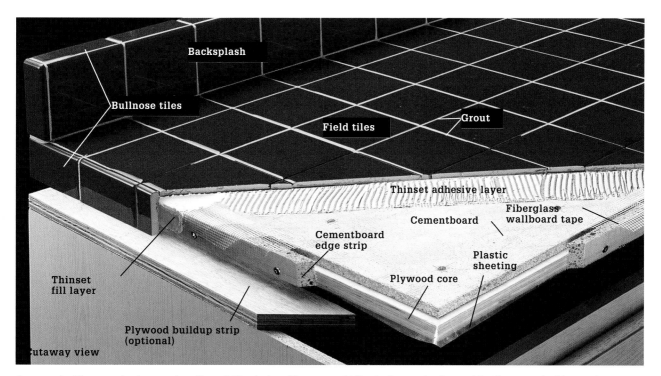

Backsplash

Bullnose tiles

Field tiles

Grout

Thinset adhesive layer

Fiberglass wallboard tape

Cementboard

Cementboard edge strip

Plastic sheeting

Plywood core

Thinset fill layer

Plywood buildup strip (optional)

Cutaway view

A ceramic tile countertop made with wall tile starts with a core of ¾" exterior-grade plywood that's covered with a moisture barrier of 4-mil polyethylene sheeting. Half-inch cementboard is screwed to the plywood, and the edges are capped with cementboard and finished with fiberglass mesh tape and thinset mortar. Tiles for edging and backsplashes may be bullnose or trimmed from the factory edges of field tiles.

Options for Backsplashes & Countertop Edges

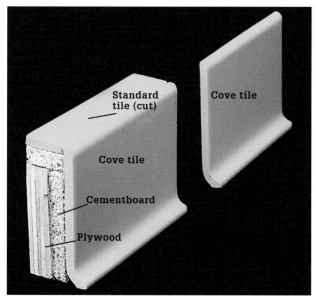

Standard tile (cut)

Cove tile

Cove tile

Cementboard

Plywood

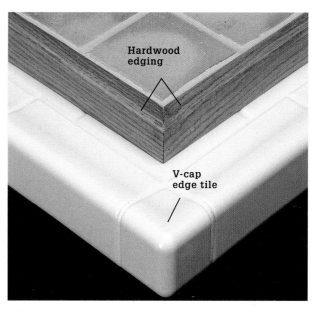

Hardwood edging

V-cap edge tile

Backsplashes can be made from cove tile attached to the wall at the back of the countertop. You can use the tile alone or build a shelf-type backsplash, using the same construction as for the countertop. Attach the plywood backsplash to the plywood core of the countertop. Wrap the front face and all edges of the plywood backsplash with cementboard before laying tile.

Edge options include V-cap edge tile and hardwood strip edging. V-cap tiles have raised and rounded corners that create a ridge around the countertop perimeter—good for containing spills and water. V-cap tiles must be cut with a tile saw. Hardwood strips should be prefinished with at least three coats of polyurethane finish. Attach the strips to the plywood core so the top of the wood will be flush with the faces of the tiles.

Tips for Laying Out Tile ▸

- You can lay tile over a laminate countertop that's square, level, and structurally sound. Use a belt sander with 60- or 80-grit sandpaper to rough up the surface before setting the tiles. The laminate cannot have a no-drip edge. If you're using a new substrate and need to remove your existing countertop, make sure the base cabinets are level front to back, side to side, and with adjoining cabinets. Unscrew a cabinet from the wall and use shims on the floor or against the wall to level it, if necessary.

- Installing battens along the front edge of the countertop helps ensure the first row of tile is perfectly straight. For V-cap tiles, fasten a 1 × 2 batten along the reference line, using screws. The first row of field tile is placed against this batten. For bullnose tiles, fasten a batten that's the same thickness as the edging tile, plus ⅛" for mortar thickness, to the face of the countertop so the top is flush with the top of the counter. The bullnose tiles are aligned with the outside edge of the batten. For wood edge trim, fasten a 1 × 2 batten to the face of the countertop so the top edge is above the top of the counter. The tiles are installed against the batten.

- Before installing any tile, lay out the tiles in a dry run using spacers. If your counter is L-shaped, start at the corner and work outward. Otherwise, start the layout at a sink to ensure equal-sized cuts on both sides of the sink. If necessary, shift your starting point so you don't end up cutting very narrow tile segments.

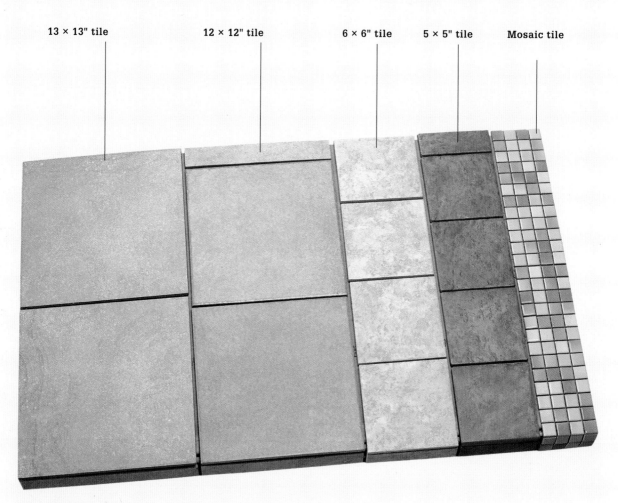

13 × 13" tile   12 × 12" tile   6 × 6" tile   5 × 5" tile   Mosaic tile

The bigger the tile the fewer the grout lines. If you want a standard 25"-deep countertop, the only way to get there without cutting tiles is to use mosaic strips or 1" tile. With 13 × 13" tile, you need to trim 1" off the back tile but have only one grout line front to back. As you decrease tile size, the number of grout lines increases.

How to Build a Tile Countertop

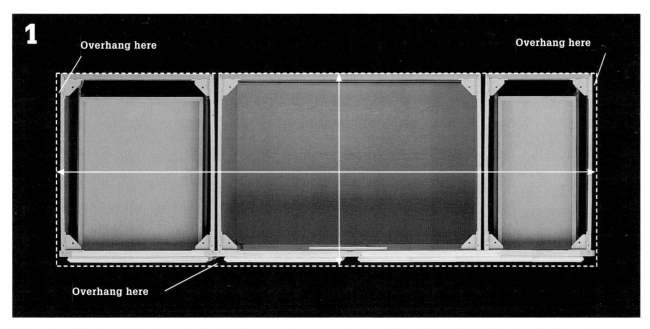

Determine the size of the plywood substrate by measuring across the top of the cabinets. The finished top should overhang the drawer fronts by at least ¼". Be sure to account for the thickness of the cementboard, adhesive, and tile when deciding how large to make the overhang. Cut the substrate to size from ¾" plywood, using a circular saw. Also make any cutouts for sinks and other fixtures.

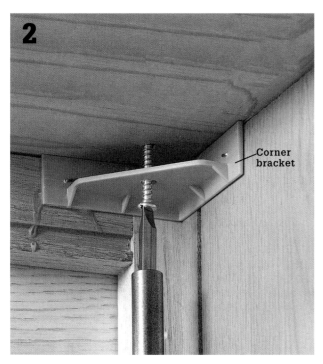

Set the plywood substrate on top of the cabinets, and attach it with screws driven through the cabinet corner brackets. The screws should not be long enough to go through the top of the substrate.

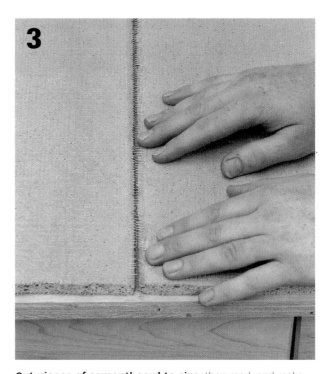

Cut pieces of cementboard to size, then mark and make the cutout for the sink. Dry-fit them on the plywood core with the rough sides of the panels facing up. Leave a ⅛" gap between the cementboard sheets and a ¼" gap along the perimeter.

(continued)

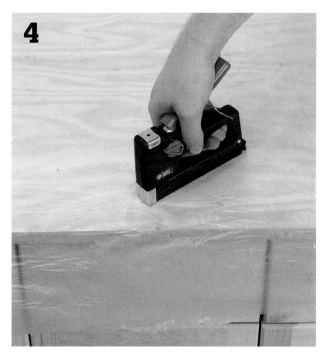

Option: Cut cementboard using a straightedge and utility knife or a cementboard cutter with a carbide tip. Hold the straightedge along the cutting line, and score the board several times with the knife. Bend the piece backward to break it along the scored line. Back-cut to finish.

Lay the 4-mil plastic moisture barrier over the plywood substrate, draping it over the edges. Tack it in place with a few staples. Overlap seams in the plastic by 6", and seal them with packing tape.

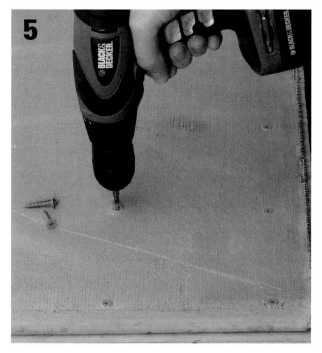

Lay the cementboard pieces rough-side up on the plywood and attach them with cementboard screws driven every 6". Drill pilot holes using a masonry bit, and make sure all screw heads are flush with the surface. Wrap the countertop edges with 1¼"-wide cementboard strips, and attach them to the core with cementboard screws.

Tape all cementboard joints with fiberglass mesh tape. Apply three layers of tape along the front edge where the horizontal cementboard sheets meet the cementboard edging.

7

Fill all gaps and cover all of the tape with a layer of thinset mortar. Feather out the mortar with a drywall knife to create a smooth, flat surface.

8

Determine the required width of your edge tiles. Lay a field tile onto the tile base so it overhangs the front edge by ½" or so. Then, hold a metal ruler up to the underside of the tile and measure the distance from the tile to the bottom of the subbase. Your edge tiles should be cut to this width. (The gap for the grout line will cause the edge tile to extend past the subbase, concealing it completely.)

9

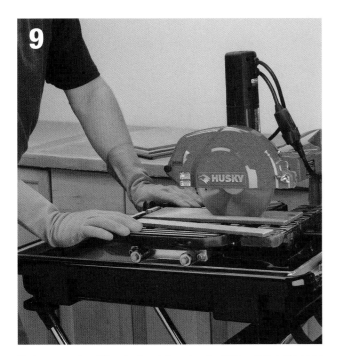

Cut your edge tiles to the determined width, using a tile saw. It's worth renting a quality wet saw for tile if you don't own one. Floor tile is thick and difficult to cut with a hand cutter (especially porcelain tiles).

10

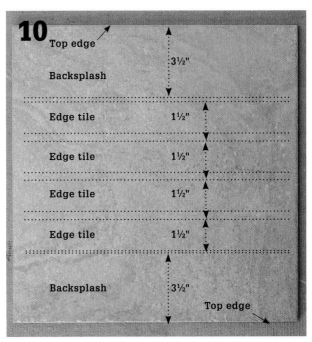

Cut tiles for the backsplash. The backsplash tiles (3½" wide in our project) should be cut with a factory edge on each tile that will be oriented upward when they're installed. You can make efficient use of your tiles by cutting edge tiles from the center area of the tiles you cut to make the backsplash.

(continued)

Sink cutout area

Dry-fit tiles on the countertop to find the layout that works best. Once the layout is established, make marks along the vertical and horizontal rows. Draw reference lines through the marks and use a framing square to make sure the lines are perpendicular.

Variation: Laying Out with Small Floor Tiles and Bullnose Edging ▶

Lay out tiles and spacers in a dry run. Adjust starting lines, if necessary. If using battens, lay the field tile flush with the battens, then apply edge tile. Otherwise, install the edging first. If the countertop has an inside corner, start there by installing a ready-made inside corner or cutting a 45° miter in edge tile to make your own inside corner.

Place the first row of field tile against the edge tile, separating the tile with spacers. Lay out the remaining rows of tile. Adjust starting lines if necessary to create a layout using the least number of cut tiles.

12

Use a ⅜" square notched trowel to apply a layer of thinset adhesive to the cementboard. Apply enough for two or three tiles, starting at one end. Hold the trowel at roughly a 30-degree angle and try not to overwork the adhesive or remove too much.

13

Set the first tile into the adhesive. Hold a piece of the edge tile against the countertop edge as a guide to show you exactly how much the tile should overhang the edge.

14

Cut all the back tiles for the layout to fit (you'll need to remove about 1" of a 13 × 13" tile) before you begin the actual installation. Set the back tiles into the thinset, maintaining the gap for groutlines created by the small spacer nubs cast into the tiles. If your tiles have no spacer nubs, see next step.

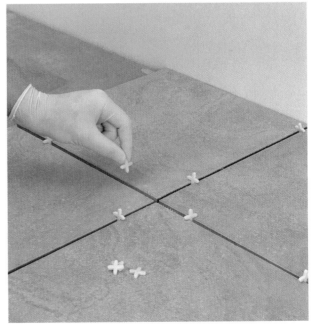

Option: To maintain even grout lines, some beginning tilers insert plus-sign shaped plastic spacers at the joints. This is less likely to be useful with large tiles like those shown here, but it is effective. Many tiles today feature built-in spacing lugs, so the spacers are of no use. Make sure to remove the spacers before the thinset sets. If you leave them in place they will corrupt your grout lines.

(continued)

Variation: To mark border tiles for cutting, allow space for backsplash tiles, grout, and mortar by placing a tile against the back wall. Set another tile (A) on top of the last full tile in the field, then place a third tile (B) over tile A and hold it against the upright tile. Mark and cut tile A and install it with the cut edge toward the wall. Finish filling in your field tiles.

To create a support ledge for the edge tiles, prop pieces of 2 × 4 underneath the front edge of the substrate overhang, using wood scraps to prop the ledge tightly up against the substrate.

Apply a thick layer of thinset to the backside of the edge tile with your trowel. This is called "buttering" and it is easier and neater than attempting to trowel adhesive onto the countertop edge. Press the tiles into position so they are flush with the leading edges of the field tiles.

Butter each backsplash tile and press it into place, doing your best to keep all of the grout lines aligned.

18

Mix a batch of grout to complement the tile (keeping in mind that darker grout won't look dirty as soon as lighter grout). Apply the grout to the grout line areas with a grout float.

19

Let the grout dry until a light film is created on the countertop surface and then wipe the excess grout off with a sponge and warm, clean water.

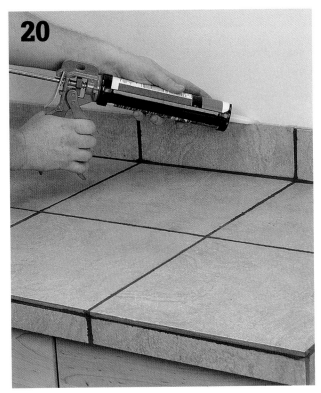

20

After the grout has dried (and before you use the sink, if possible) run a bead of clear silicone caulk along the joint between the backsplash and the wall. Install your sink and faucet.

21

Wait at least one week and then seal the grout lines with a penetrating grout sealer. This is important to do. Sealing the tiles themselves is not a good idea unless you are using unglazed tiles (a poor choice for countertops, however).

21. Tiling Concrete Steps

In addition to the traditional tricks for improving your home's curb appeal—landscaping, fresh paint, pretty windows—a tiled entry makes a wonderful, positive impression. To be suitable for tiling, stair treads must be deep enough to walk on safely. Check local building codes for specifics, but most require that treads be at least 11" deep (from front to back) after the tile is added.

Before you start laying any tiles, the concrete must be free of curing agents, clean, and in good shape. Make necessary repairs and give them time to cure. An isolation membrane can be applied before the tile. This membrane can be a fiberglass sheet or it can be brushed on as a liquid to dry. In either case, it separates the tile from the concrete, which allows the two to move independently and protects the tile from potential settling or shifting of the concrete.

Choose exterior-rated, unglazed floor tile with a skid-resistant surface. Tile for the walking surfaces should be at least ½" thick. Use bullnose tiles at the front edges of treads (as you would on a countertop) and use cove tiles as the bottom course on risers.

Tools & Materials ▸

Pressure washer
Masonry trowel
4-foot level
Carpenter's square
Straightedge
Tape measure
Chalk line
Tile cutter or wet saw
Tile nippers
Square-notched trowel
Needle-nose plier
Rubber mallet
Grout float
Grout sponge
Caulk gun
Latex or epoxy patching compound
Isolation membrane

Tile spacers
Buckets
Paintbrush and roller
Plastic sheeting
Paper towels
Dry-set mortar
Field tile
Bullnose tile
Grout
Grout additive
Latex tile caulk
Grout sealer
Tile sealer
2 × 4
Carpet scrap
Cold chisel or flat-head screwdriver
Wire brush
Broom

How to Tile Concrete Steps

Use a pressure washer to clean the surface of the concrete. (Use a washer with at least 4,000 psi and follow manufacturer's instructions carefully to avoid damaging the concrete with the pressurized spray.)

Dig out rubble in large cracks and chips, using a small cold chisel or flat-head screwdriver. Use a wire brush to loosen dirt and debris in small cracks. Sweep the area or use a wet/dry vacuum to remove all debris.

Fill small cracks and chips with masonry patching compound, using a masonry trowel. Allow the patching compound to cure according to manufacturer's directions.

If damage is located at a front edge, clean it as described above. Place a board in front and block the board in place with bricks or concrete blocks. Wet the damaged area and fill it with patching compound. Use a masonry trowel to smooth the patch and then allow it to cure thoroughly.

Test the surface of the steps and stoop for low spots, using a 4-foot level or other straightedge. Fill any low spots with patching compound and allow the compound to cure thoroughly.

(continued)

Spread a layer of isolation membrane over the concrete, using a notched trowel. Smooth the surface of the membrane, using the flat edge of a trowel. Allow the membrane to cure according to manufacturer's directions.

The sequence is important when tiling a stairway with landing. The primary objective is to install the tile in such a way that the fewest possible cut edges are visible from the main viewing position. If you are tiling the sides of concrete steps, start laying tile there first. Begin by extending horizontal lines from the tops of the stair treads back to the house on the sides of the steps. Use a 4-foot level.

Mix a batch of thinset mortar with latex bonding adhesive and trowel it onto the sides of the steps, trying to retain visibility of the layout lines. Because the top steps are likely more visible than the bottom steps, start on top and work your way down.

Begin setting tiles into the thinset mortar on the sides of the steps. Start at the top and work your way downward. Try to lay out tile so the vertical gaps between tiles align. Use spacers if you need to.

Wrap a 2 × 4 in old carpet and drag it back and forth across the tile surfaces to set them evenly. Don't get too aggressive here—you don't want to dislodge all of the thinset mortar.

Measure the width of a riser, including the thickness of the tiles you've laid on the step sides. Calculate the centerpoint and mark it clearly with chalk or a high visibility marker.

Next, install the tiles on the stair risers. Because the location of the tops of the riser tiles affects the positioning of the tread and landing tiles, you'll get the most accurate layout if the riser tiles are laid first. Start by stacking tiles vertically against the riser. (In some cases, you'll only need one tile to reach from tread to tread.) Add spacers. Trace the location of the tread across the back of the top tile to mark it for cutting.

Cut enough tiles to size to lay tiles for all the stair risers. Be sure to allow enough space for grout joints if you are stacking tiles.

Trowel thinset mortar mixed with bonding adhesive onto the faces of the risers. In most cases, you should be able to tile each riser all at once.

Lay tiles on the risers. The bottom tile edges can rest on the tread, and the tops of the top tiles should be flush with or slightly lower than the plane of the tread above.

(continued)

Dry-lay tile in both directions on the stair landing. You'll want to maintain the same grout lines that are established by the riser tiles, but you'll want to evaluate the front-to-back layout to make sure you don't end up with a row of tiles that is less than 2" or so in thickness.

Cut tiles as indicated by your dry run, and then begin installing them by troweling thinset adhesive for the bullnose tiles at the front edge of the landing. The tiles should overlap the top edges of the riser tiles, but not extend past their faces.

Field tile

Bullnose tile

Set the first row of field tiles, maintaining an even gap between the field tiles and the bullnose tiles.

Add the last row of tiles next to the house and threshold, cutting them as needed so they are between ¼" and ½" away from the house.

Install tiles on the stair treads, starting at the top tread and working your way downward. Set a bullnose tile on each side of the centerline and work your way toward the sides, making sure to conceal the step side tiles with the tread tiles.

Fill in the field tiles on the stair treads, being sure to leave a gap between the back tiles and the riser tiles that's the same thickness as the other tile gaps.

Let the thinset mortar cure for a few days, and then apply grout in the gaps between tiles using a grout float. Wipe away the grout after it clouds over. Cover with plastic, in the event of rain.

After a few weeks, seal the grout lines with an exterior-rated grout sealer.

Select (or have prepared) a pretinted caulk that's the same color as your grout. Fill the gap between the back row of tiles and the house with caulk. Smooth with a wet finger if needed.

Glossary

American National Standards Institute (ANSI): A standards-making organization that rates tile for water permeability.

Art tiles: Hand-finished tiles with designs, pictures, or patterns. Art tiles are often used to accent a large tile layout.

Back buttering: Spreading mortar on the back of a tile before pressing it onto the substrate.

Baseboard tile: Baseboard-shaped tiles used to replace wood baseboards.

Bullnose trim tile: Tile with one rounded edge that is meant to be left exposed.

Cement body tile: Tile made from concrete poured into forms.

Coefficient of friction: The measure of a tile's slip resistance. Tiles with high numbers are more slip-resistant.

Decorative: Tile with designs, pictures, or relief. Decorative tiles are generally used as accents in a field of solid-color tiles.

Dry fit: Installing tile without mortar in order to test the layout.

Expansion joint: An expansion joint is a joint in a tile layout filled with a flexible material like caulk instead of grout. The expansion joint allows the tile to shift without cracking.

Field tiles: The main tile in a tile design. As opposed to trim or accent tiles.

Floor tile: Any type of tile designated for use on floors. It can generally also be used for walls or countertops.

Floor-warming systems: A system of heating elements installed directly under the floor material. Floor-warming systems are intended to provide supplemental radiant heat for a room.

Glass tile: Tile made of translucent glass. Glass tile is often used as accent tile.

Glazed ceramic: Tile made from refined clay that has been coated with a glaze and then fired in a kiln.

Grade: Ratings applied to some tile indicating the quality and consistency of manufacturing. Grade 1 tile is standard, suitable for most applications; grade 2 may have minor glaze and size imperfections; grade 3 tile is thin and suitable only for wall or decorative applications.

Grout: A dry powder, usually cement based, that is mixed with water and pressed into the joints between tiles. Grout also comes with latex or acrylic added for greater adhesion and impermeability.

Impervious: Tile that absorbs less than .5% of its weight in water.

Isolation membrane: Isolation membrane is a flexible material installed in sheets or troweled onto an unstable or damaged base floor, subfloor, or wall before installing tile. The isolation membrane prevents shifts in the base from damaging the tile above.

Joists: The framing members that support the floor.

Kiln: A high-temperature oven used to harden clay tile.

Liners: Narrow tiles used for adding contrasting lines to tile layouts.

Listello: A border tile, usually with a raised design. Also called listel.

Mastic or organic mastic: A type of glue for installing tile. It comes premixed and cures as it dries. It is convenient for wall tiles smaller than 6 × 6, but it is not suitable for floors.

Metal tile: Tile made of iron, stainless steel, copper, or brass. Metal tile is often used as accent tile.

Mortar or thinset mortar: A mixture of portland cement and sand and occasionally a latex or acrylic additive to improve adhesion.

Mosaic tile: Small colored tiles used to make patterns or pictures on walls and floors.

Natural stone tile: Tile cut from marble, slate, granite, or other natural stone.

Non-vitreous: Very permeable tile. Non-vitreous tile absorbs more than 7% of its total weight in water. Not suitable for outdoor installations.

Porcelain Enamel Institute (PEI): A tile industry group that issues ratings on tile's resistance to wear.

Porcelain tile: Tile made from refined white clay fired at high temperatures. Porcelain is usually dyed rather than glazed, and thus its color runs the tile's full thickness.

Quarry tile: Tile formed to look like quarried stone.

Reference lines: Lines marked on the substrate to guide the placement of the first row of tile.

Saltillo: Terra-cotta tile from Mexico. Saltillos have a distinctly rustic appearance.

Sealants: Sealants protect non- and semi-vitreous tile from stains and from water damage. Sealants are also important for protecting grout.

Self-spacing tile: Tile with attached tabs for maintaining even spacing.

Semi-vitreous: Moderately permeable tile. Absorbs 3-7% of its total weight in water. Not suitable for outdoor installations.

Spacers: Plastic lugs meant to be inserted between tiles to help maintain uniform spacing during installation.

Story stick: A length of 1×2 lumbar marked with the tile spacing for a specific layout.

Subfloor: The surface, usually made of plywood, attached to the floor joists.

Substrates or underlayment: A surface installed on top of an existing floor, subfloor, or wall. The substrate creates a suitable surface for installing tile. Substrate materials include cementboard, plywood, cork, backerboard, greenboard, or water-proofing membrane.

Terra-cotta tile: Tile made from unrefined clay. Terra-cotta is fired at low temperature. Its color varies greatly depending on where the source of the clay.

Trim tile: Tile with a finished edge for completing wall tile layouts.

V-cap tiles: V- or L-shaped tile for finishing the exposed edges of countertops.

Vitreous: Slightly permeable tile. Absorbs .5-3% of its total weight in water.

Wall tile: Tile intended for use on walls. It is generally thinner than floor tile and should not be used on floors or countertops.

Water absorption or permeability: The measure of the amount of water that will penetrate a tile when it is wet. Measurement ranges from non-vitreous to semi-vitreous to vitreous to impervious.

Waterproofing membrane: A flexible, water-proof material installed in sheets or brushed on to protect the subfloor from water damage.

Creative Publishing international

Here's How Ceramic Tile
Created by: The Editors of Creative Publishing international, Inc., in cooperation with Black & Decker. Black & Decker® is a trademark of The Black & Decker Corporation and is used under license.

President/CEO: Ken Fund
VP for Sales & Marketing: Kevin Hamric

Home Improvement Group

Publisher: Bryan Trandem
Managing Editor: Tracy Stanley
Senior Editor: Mark Johanson
Editor: Jennifer Gehlhar

Creative Director: Michele Lanci-Altomare
Senior Design Managers: Jon Simpson, Brad Springer
Design Manager: James Kegley

Lead Photographer: Joel Schnell

Production Managers: Linda Halls, Laura Hokkanen

Page Layout Artist: Danielle Smith

NOTICE TO READERS

For safety, use caution, care, and good judgment when following the procedures described in this book. The publisher and Black & Decker cannot assume responsibility for any damage to property or injury to persons as a result of misuse of the information provided.

The techniques shown in this book are general techniques for various applications. In some instances, additional techniques not shown in this book may be required. Always follow manufacturers' instructions included with products, since deviating from the directions may void warranties. The projects in this book vary widely as to skill levels required: some may not be appropriate for all do-it-yourselfers, and some may require professional help.

Consult your local building department for information on building permits, codes, and other laws as they apply to your project.